Dedication

When I think of Heaven, I think of those who have gone before us. I think of all the trials they endured and the examples they left for us. Being in this place of life where I have as many waiting on the other side as I do here on Earth, Heaven is sounding much sweeter all the time! To all who have run this race and finished the course before us, this devotional is dedicated to you.

To my precious Daddy, thank you for teaching me to cherish the gems of His word as the most precious of life's gifts.

"God's Word is better than a diamond, better than a diamond set between emeralds."
Psalms 19:10 MSG

Puddles of Diamonds from Heaven

Reflections of God Moments Collection 3
56 One Minute Devotionals

Written by: Donesa Walker
Design by: Will Baten

Table of Contents

Post this at all the intersections, dear friends: Lead with your ears, follow up with your tongue, and let anger straggle along in the rear.

God's righteousness doesn't grow from human anger. So throw all spoiled virtue and cancerous evil in the garbage. In simple humility, let our gardener, God, landscape you with the Word, making a salvation-garden of your life.

James 1:19-21

Listening Landscape!

Recently Wes and I set out to prune back the plants in our yard as we do each year. I am an untrained gardener, but he knows his stuff. He quickly goes about the cutting and honestly it looks weird because he doesn't cut back evenly. Some parts of the bush are taller, other shorter, some nonexistent. Finally, after puzzling why he was doing it that way, I asked. He said something about five and growth and such which I completely didn't understand. I decided I better just sit back and listen because he's the one who knows. Every year our rose bushes bloom gloriously twice.

Then it was time to pick up the extra clippings, again I was instructed to do so with proper tools because you don't want to transfer dead growth or disease to the freshly trimmed bush. Truthfully not a lot of this made sense to me but I know he knows what he is doing because I've watched these bushes bloom beautifully for over ten years getting prettier and more vibrant every year. God's righteousness doesn't grow from weeds or diseased trimmings. His glory doesn't come from anger, harsh words, or negative doubt. God's glory and fruitfulness in us comes from simple humility and yielding our desires to His. God landscapes us the Master Gardener with His word, but we must be willing to listen and hear with our whole heart. The salvation garden like my garden of roses requires pruning that is often painful and ugly but necessary to our overall growth.

James tells us to post this everywhere so we will be reminded to lead with our ears and not our tongue. He wants us to not give reign to our anger and frustration but rather to lean into the Master Gardener with trust that He knows what is best. The blooms have already begun on the roses that were pruned. The beautiful maroon leaves of new growth have covered the bare branches and as the sun reflects over the water, I see the reflection of the rose and realize that listening to the voice of the one who knows my tomorrow is much more important than my tantrum at my frustration of things not going my way. God the master gardener has a plan if I will tame my tongue, harness my anger, and become the listening landscape under his guidance.

I looked again. I saw a huge crowd, too huge to count. Everyone was there all nations and tribes, all races and languages. And they were standing, dressed in white robes and waving palm branches, standing before the Throne and the Lamb and heartily singing: Salvation to our God on his Throne! Salvation to the Lamb! All who were standing around the Throne-Angels, Elders, Animals--fell on their faces before the Throne and worshiped God, singing Oh, Yes! The blessing and glory and wisdom and thanksgiving, The honor and power and strength, To our God forever and ever and ever! Oh, Yes!
Revelation 7:9-12

The Unseen Glory!

John writes Revelation from exile on the Isle of Patmos. There, where he is being punished by the powers that were, He encountered the I Am who will always be. The hidden things of God can only be seen when we let go of what is. Reality is fleeting and only exists as a possibility of what could be. Each moment has the opportunity to be more than just a second in time if you seek the truth. These beautiful mushrooms are one example. The fungi are always there as a network underground that does many things necessary for nature to thrive but only in times of excess rain do we see the evidence of them flowering into our vision. Some of these are extremely dangerous to us, some are greatly beneficial to us, and some are just a part of the network of life but still integral to our world. It takes a particular set of circumstances for them to be revealed and such is the hidden truths of God.

The blessings, the glory, the wisdom, the thanksgiving, the honor, the power, and the strength all belong to God forever and ever. Yet, it took John in a particular time and place of circumstances to understand this about God and to reveal the truth that ALL will recognize this, at the Throne of God and The Lamb: Jesus who takes away the veil. This huge crowd recognizes who He is more than ever before...as one. We are all one. We are His sheep of His pasture and each of us willfully goes his/her own way but softly and gently He woos us back through our circumstances of life to see the truth being revealed in us. What is it that you are hiding that will be revealed? Is it something dangerous and deadly to your soul? Is it something beautiful and wondrous that is beneficial to all? All that is hidden will be known. And no matter who or what you are, you will bow to the name above all names, Jesus Christ.

The circumstances may be right today to reveal your hidden depths or today may be the day you develop the things that profoundly change the network of your life. You have a choice. He's always there. You may choose to plug into the network of Life and allow your circumstances to reveal your hidden depths and beauty or you can remain hidden until the circumstances cause you to reveal your truth. The Unseen Glory is a taste of Heaven. Oh Yes, oh yes, I am a child of the king...His royal blood does flow through my veins...

Halleluiah! It's a good thing to sing praise to our God; praise isbeautiful, praise is fitting. God's the one who rebuilds Jerusalem, who regathers Israel's scattered exiles. He heals the heartbroken and bandages their wounds. He counts the stars and assigns each a name. Our Lord is great, with limitless strength; we'll never comprehend what he knows and does. God puts the fallen on their feet again and pushes the wicked into the ditch. Sing to God a thanksgiving hymn, play music on your instruments to God, Who fills the sky with clouds, preparing rainfor the earth, Then turning themountains green with grass, feeding both cattle and crows.He's not impressed with horsepower the size of our muscles means little to him. Those who fearGod get God's attention; they Can depend on his strength.
Psalms 147:1-11

Limitless attention!

In a world where our attention is less than that of a goldfish, it is good to know that God is not subject to our follies. His limitless strength is not subject to our attention span, but He counts the stars and knows them by name. He knows us intimately as we enter into His presence and His rest through praise. God's the one who does it all. There is no problem so big that God cannot solve. It is beyond our comprehension, but it is not beyond our ability to praise through it. I see people and hear of people spending thousands of dollars and endless amounts of time praising sports stars, singers, and movie stars. Our society is filled with a clamor for fame and fortune through whatever means they can get attention without realizing that they already have the attention of the most important person of all just through a whisper or a breath. His very breath flows through us, and He hears us as we move.

He moves within us quietly and magnificently if we would but calm ourselves and feel Him. There is nothing that impresses Him in strength of man or feat, not the biggest engine or the mightiest machine. All is wasteful and done at the breath of praise. A small cry in the womb from an injured child carries more weight than the loudest proclamation of the highest authority in Earth, as He is not subject to any man. While one may not recognize who He is; all are subject to what He does. Our Lord is great and worthy of praise. It is He who set the world in motion. There is no agenda more powerful than His, nor any means stronger than Him. His strength is ours, just as we move in Him. The fear of God is the most unlimited place of praise. The knowing. Singing to God, worshiping God, praising God all are but ways to openly acknowledge the fear/respect for who He is. Rulers come and go in this world. Their reigns are finite and subject to His allowances.

Their power is nothing compared to the power of a child's cry in sincerity to God Himself. Imagine it. You have the limitless attention of a God whose strength cannot be matched, whose power cannot be overwhelmed and whose knowledge is so vast, none can harness it. And you have His attention at the whisper of His name.

So if you're serious about living this new resurrection life with Christ, act like it. Pursue the things over which Christ presides. Don't shuffle along, eyes to the ground, absorbed with the things right in front of you. Look up, and be alert to what is going on around Christ-that's where the action is. See things from his perspective. Your old life is dead. Your new life, which is your real life even though invisible to spectators is with Christ in God. He is your life.When Christ (your real life, remember) shows up again on this earth, you'll show up, too-the real you, the glorious you. Meanwhile, be content with obscurity, like Christ.
Colossians 3:1-4

The REAL you!

Pursuit. What are you pursuing? In Colossians, we learn that these people were actively walking around trying to hide who they were in fear or absorbed with things in their everyday life not realizing their true purpose. Missing the action and seeing things from a worldly stage is depressing and pointless. My Papaw had a favorite saying, "Look up and Be sweet". It's what he said every time I saw him. Here the instructions are Look up and Be alert! Christ and all that is in Him is where the action is, the real life, the excitement, the REALITY. Your real life may be invisible to those who cannot see through eyes of God, but it is your real life. Pursue His glory for that is where your REAL you are at, not in the things of Earth. Don't get absorbed with the temporary but focus on the eternal. Don't be beat down, eyes to ground or poor me, my life stinks...Look UP!

Look up, be sweet and Be alert! The signs of the times are everywhere! The other day I was in the pool doing some aerobic exercises with some friends and we were discussing the signs of the times when suddenly I looked up...and the most beautiful rainbow was there! His promises...that's where we look. Don't get discouraged by the symptoms of an Earth groaning in preparation as a mother about to give birth...the birth pangs signal His return so Look UP! Get your eyes off the things that fade and Look to the things which are eternal. Does this mean we stop functioning in life? Absolutely not! You're the only Jesus some people will ever see....so who are they seeing?

When you represent someone whether that be your family, your boss, your business or other...it should be the best you there is...if you are representing Jesus Christ who died for all and is here in you to give life to all...let Him live through you! Be the Jesus, He wants you to be. Allow His invisible presence to flow through you as a fragrance and let the room know someone important is there; it's not you but Him. Let them feel Him in your behavior and presence. He is your true life. Until He comes again in His glorious return to Earth, He is your life. Be content in representing who He is! If you're serious about living the resurrection life of Christ, then act like it! Pursue Him and the things of His purpose. See things from His perspective. It's not your legacy but His name that matters. What are you pursuing?

How can a young person live a clean life? By carefully reading the map of your Word. I'm single-minded in pursuit of you; don't let me miss the road signs you've posted. I've banked your promises in the vault of my heart so I won't sin myself bankrupt. Be blessed, God; train me in your ways of wise living.
I'll transfer to my lips all the counsel that comes from your mouth; I delight far more in what you tell me about living than in gathering a pile of riches. I ponder every morsel of wisdom from you, I attentively watch how you've done it. I relish everything you've told me of life, I won't forget a word of it.

* * *

Psalms 119:9-16

Reading The Treasure Map!

Reading is a pastime I enjoy especially when it is a mystery book. Reading the Bible is like a magically treasure hunt for the morsels of wisdom that God drops into the vault of our hearts. David, the Psalmist, says living a clean life is achieved by reading the map of God's word.

A treasure hunter is not double minded but rather singularly focused so that no clue us missed while searching. I grew up in the Indiana Jones era where the mystery of the Lost Ark was the goal...or the Holy Grail. These artifacts of priceless value led the researcher/ archeologists on treasure hunts through dangerous places risking everything to find the priceless treasure. Lots of movies and books have been filmed and written about the hidden priceless treasures that people search for in pursuit of fame, wealth, and acknowledgment but few ever realized that each person has access if they will but singularly pursue God. Psalms 119 is a treasure map of unbridled wealth of knowledge in the hunt.

When one sets off on a treasure hunt, the person must carefully read and search text for clues and dive deep into research for that nugget of truth hidden among the texts. They must learn, glean, and carefully bank what they learn to ponder it in the vault of their hearts and minds watching for clues and signs that it us time to use that knowledge. This requires diligence and training. When that nugget of knowledge springs forth in that prime moment to your lips, you know the treasure that is more valuable than any riches on Earth. In a society fraught with attentional distractions from the pondering of His word, many miss the treasure. Memories are made from small moments of tuning in and pondering or relishing that experience. The treasure map to true living in here in this passage. Can you find it? Jesus says...You shall find me when you seek me with all of your heart, soul, mind, and strength. Are you spiritually bankrupt, searching for your next source of provision? It's here. Look, seek, find, and bank the treasure for use in His time.

"Are you tired? Worn out? Burned out on religion? Come to me. Get away with me and you'll recover your life. I'll show you how to take a real rest. Walk with me and work with me-watch how I do it. Learn the unforced rhythms of grace. I won't lay anything heavy or ill-fitting on you. Keep company with me and you'll learn to live freely and lightly." Matthew 11:28-30

Rhythms of Grace!

In a world weighty with opinions and performance, it gets tiring trying to keep up. Our bodies and our souls become weary. We get easily discouraged and beat down by the stress of trying to live up to expectations and yet, that is not the path God created for us. He beckons us into His living rest. I've heard lots of people say that they'll rest when they get to Heaven but right now is time to work...that doesn't align with scripture. Jesus knew this. In the Book of Matthew, he records Jesus' words as he speaks to those weary of their lot in life. "are you tired? Worn out? Burned out? Come to me!" Jesus wants you to escape to Him.

Television, social media, video games, books, entertainment of all kinds have become our getaway but in these we have mindlessness not rest. True rest...the kind our bodies and minds need doesn't come from vacations and getaways like we think. Real rest comes from Him. It's unforced. I'm always amazed as fall approaches and the breeze begins to blow while the trees carelessly shed their leaves. It's a crisp day with leaves turning as they prepare to let go and fall into nothingness or the unknown which becomes life. Living that freely and lightly as a leaf on a tree that takes in the sunlight and rain, flutters in the breezes and endures the scorching rays of heat for the sole purpose of the tree is what we are called to do. Jesus calls it the rhythms of grace. He said we learn them by keeping company with Him. He said to walk with Him, work with Him and watch How He does it. But how? I mean in Matthew's time, Jesus literally walked with Him so how do I today see how He does it? The truth is that now He lives in us, with us and directs us if we listen.

The Rhythm of Grace is in you. The ability to achieve true rest is in you but you must take the time away to walk with Him and keep company with Him. You must learn to tune yourself to His voice and hear His rhythm just as the leaves know when to let go and trust... you must learn when to let go and trust His grace. Are you carrying a burden that seems too hard to bear? Give it to Jesus and leave it there. Feeling like you are hopeless and discouraged with so many uncertainties of your future and your dreams? Take it Jesus. Take a walk with Him through His word. Let His rhythm infuses you with His grace and lift that burden. It doesn't happen overnight as it is a lesson of learning to live freely, lightly, unencumbered with the cares of life. Get away with Him and recover your life.

If you love learning, you love the discipline that goes with it- how shortsighted to refuse correction! You can't find firm footing in a swamp, but life rooted in God stands firm. The thinking of principled people makes for justice; the plots of degenerates corrupt. Well-spoken words bring satisfaction; well-done work has its own reward. Fools have short fuses and explode all too quickly; the prudent quietly shrug off insults. Truth lasts; lies are here today, gone tomorrow.Worry weighs us down; a cheerful word picks us up.
Proverbs 12:1, 3, 5, 14, 16, 19, 25

Rooted in Truth!

As a teacher by heart and trade, I love learning. But a classroom of unruliness is not fun and requires discipline to set it straight because true learning cannot take place in chaos. The brain requires organized thoughts to acquire and file the memories. Discipline requires course correction. If you are not rooted in truth, then it is like quicksand or a mucky swamp. It sucks one down into the depth of it choking out the life. Principles that are fixed are look roots that hold you strong when the swampy murky waters of corruption tear at the core of the fabric. Lies that tear down, disrupt and pull are the murkiness of this corrupted society. The media spin and sensationalization of things that are half-truths or outright lies is incredible. But we as God's people must stay rooted in truth and not let emotions sway us in unprincipled chaos. The instructions of doing decent work and well-spoken words comes from not allowing the emotions to rage. Emotions swap you into short tempered explosions and downhearted negativity instead of seeing His true purpose. Emotions lead us into places of insecurity and worry.

Worry weighs us down. We must choose to walk in His light and wisdom even when the people around us fail us. Truth lasts. It's a tap root. A tap root on a tree is a central root that goes deep into the foundations of the earth and draws water when none is to be had on the surface. When things are incredibly dry around you and people desert you emotionally or fail to live up to your expectations of them, you can easily be tossed around by the chaos of emotion and worry but if your tap root is deep in God's principles then even when there is no life around you and all seems rocky and harsh, you will stand strong in God's truth and principles. This is the wisdom of Solomon given by God.

Life rooted in God stands firm through every test of life. Harsh words, evil intentions, lack of care, un-principled behaviors, shortsightedness, etc. have no ability to tear at you causing worry if you are rooted deep. Don't be fearful of the pruning. The pruning allows the tap root to go deeper because it takes off the dross or extra unnecessary froth that sits on the surface. Learning these things isn't always easy. It requires discipline through God's intervention in our lives. Training and teaching only come when the structure and rules are set and followed. Begin by disciplining your life through His word. Set time aside to prioritize Him. Put His princi-ples into practice from tithing to devotionals, worship to service, and praying to believing. Root.
Rooting requires digging deep and growing in Him often in the dark times. The seed becomes nothing lest it first die to itself in the depths of darkness. It must settle into the soil so it may push through to the light and be-come what it is intended to be. If it tries to grow upwards before rooting, it will die at the first test of the heat. If one doesn't tap deep into His living water then when the harshness of the elements of life assails you, you will shrivel up and become a bitter unfruitful dying person froth with anger and resentment that strikes out at those around you. God's love is deep. It is a source that never runs dry and when circumstances of life come, the tap root gives life even against the harshness of the ax. The tap root unless it is dug up will reroot new growth even if the tree is cut completely apart. Root! Grow deep in Him.

How blessed the man you train, God, the woman you instruct in your Word, Providing a circle of quiet within the clamor of evil, while a jail is being built for the wicked. God will never walk away from his people, never desert his precious people. Rest assured that justice is on its way and every good heart put right. Who stood up for me against the wicked? Who took my side against evil workers? If God hadn't been there for me, I never would have made it. The minute I said, "I'm slipping, I'm falling," your love, God, took hold and held me fast. When I was upset and beside myself, you calmed me down and cheered me up.

Psalms 94:12-19

Held fast!

The blessing of the anchor in the storm is not that the storm doesn't come but that peace comes along with it. David called it a circle of quiet in the clamor of evil. My mom told me it is completed confidence that God is with you despite the circumstances. Each person has their own definitions of that anchor to them but the anchor itself is His word. When the storm breaks around you, in you, above you...the knowledge of the word hidden in your heart gives you the ability to withstand. God never walks away or deserts His people. When evil strikes, God arises and shields us from the fiery darts that would destroy our souls. I can tell you about the place of slipping and not understanding where God is...when you feel that you cannot see Him, He's the knot at the end of the rope holding you.
There's a famous poem called Footprints that I've often read, and it says that God carries us through the tough times. But how can I say "uncle", "enough", "I cannot take anymore"? God hears our cries of our hearts. When I get upset and beside myself-out of my mind with grief, pain, or frustration at my own inability...I call out to Him and He hears me. His love surrounds us in the deepest waters. When you find the depths of His love, the storm has no fear anymore because His perfect love casts it out.

Isaiah 43:2 When you pass through the waters, I will be with you; and when you pass through the rivers, they will not sweep over you. When you walk through the fire, you will not be burned; the flames will not set you ablaze. The thing to remember in the hardest places is that He is there. Lean in. Press in. He knows your name. He allowed that storm for whatever purpose. Rise up in Him knowing that He has you. I picture a Hurricane swelling and rising with raging winds, but He is the quiet in it. Whether you are under attack of evil now or fighting against illness, disease or other things, God says to you-The storms know my voice and my voice walks within you. Grasp that. If He can speak to that storm to be still then through Him, so can you. No matter your situation, grief, pain, or attack, rise up and let Him work a mighty redemption in you.

Worship brings victory! There's power in praise...it breaks up jail cells, releases bondage and heals! Lift a voice! Rise up! with the cares of life. Get away with Him and recover your life.

Have I not commanded you? Be strong and courageous. Do not be afraid; do not be discouraged, for the Lord your God will be with you wherever you go.
Joshua 1:9

Be Strong and Courageous!

Strength and courage sound the same, but they are not. Courage is a step above. It is strength during adversity. Strength is the ability to withstand intense pressure. God is our strength means He is our ability...but the courage is the will to allow Him to be our strength in our weakness. Giving everything, you have and allowing God to take that amount to make it into mightiness is the courage-the strength in face of adversity. Joshua was discouraged after the death of Moses. God had called him to lead the people, but he felt inadequate and unable. So, God gave him a pep talk. Joshua 1:1-9 is God's pep talk to Joshua, and it is to us when we are feeling down or discouraged.

All your life-when you are in God-no one can hold out against you! God says He won't give up on you! He won't leave you! He'll be with you every step of the way. He commands us to take heart, be strong, be courageous! Lean into His promises with all our hearts and souls. Keep His word on our hearts and minds-pondering it...meditating on it and practicing it because that's the secret to success. Not fear but boldness. Not discouraged but secure in His promises.

His path may have twists and turns that are unexpected and even scary but if we lean in, they can be thrilling rather than terrifying. Life is a roller coaster. It has loops and turns, difficulties. It has shock waves and unexpected drops as well unexpected highs. Oftentimes this can be overwhelming and completely overstimulating. But God....read His promises... steep in them...He is with you. He is your strength!

The payoff for meekness and Fear-of-God is plenty and honor and a satisfying life. God loves the pure-hearted and well-spoken; good leaders also delight in their friendship. God guards knowledge with a passion, but he'll have nothing to do with deception. Listen carefully to my wisdom; take to heart what I can teach you. You'll treasure its sweetness deep within; you'll give it bold expression in your speech. To make sure your foundation is trust in God, I'm laying it all out right now just for you. I'm giving you sterling principles- tested guidelines to live by. Believe me these are truths that work, and will keep you accountable to those who sent you.
Proverbs 22:4,
11-12, 17-21

Tested Guidelines!

Pouring concrete without a tensile strengthening to keep it from breaking risks your foundation to cracking. The rebar is put in to give the concrete support and strength like the sterling in silver. Silver is too soft by itself to be used in usable ways, but sterling silver is strengthened by other metals like copper to give it more tenacity for long term use. Accountability to others is the same. I hear many say that they don't need to go to church or be around other Christians, but this is counter to the principles that God set forth because He knows that support in our lives is critical to our beings. God loves the pure of spirit and meekness, respect and well-spoken people and rewards them with plenty, honor and a satisfying life but He also gives wisdom, knowledge and strong truths to live by which are the sterling principles, the bold expression of speech and the tensile strength to mold this life into a usable force of His glory. It's the balance of His strength in my weakness that makes me usable for His glory.

The hard truths that dwell in scripture that many in the church have refused to dwell by are what gives the support to the framework. It may make you uncomfortable that these principles exist, but these truths are the bedrock to the foundation. If you are looking for foundational principles to guide you in uncertain circumstances, look to His word. His word lives and breathes authority and has stood the test of time. It will not be shaken when all else will be. The purpose to a durable foundation is that it can be relied on to be there through all storms. It is the guideline to the rest of the house. It is tested and true. You can treasure it knowing its value is strong, solid, and true. Fads come and go, quirky sayings, mottos, movements but the Word never fails or changes. Solid, stable, dependable, and everlasting as He is because His word is life.

So don't lose a minute in building on what you've been given, complementing your basic faith with good character, spiritual understanding, alert discipline, passionate patience, reverent wonder, warm friendliness, and generous love, each dimension fitting into and developing the others. With these qualities active and growing in your lives, no grass will grow under your feet, no day will pass without its reward as you mature in your experience of our Master Jesus. Without these qualities you can't see what's right before you, oblivious that your old sinful life has been wiped off the books.

2 Peter 1:5-9

Dimensions of Glory!

As aging occurs, seeing things with clarity is harder without the assistance of glasses. The reason is because the lenses of our natural eye get less flexible and more rigid just like other parts of our body. Seeing a 3D movie requires special glasses also because the movie is filmed in layers to give it a realistic manner just like many of the VR games now available where you can feel like you are in the game itself via a headset. All of these extra types of viewing require a special set of glasses/lenses/headsets...

As we grow and mature in the walk with Christ, we must begin to build on the basic saving faith that brought us into the relationship. The building blocks require work or extra tools to see things differently than worldview. Peter suggests that we start with good character for this is reflection of who Christ Jesus is in us. So, the building looks like a fortress of reliable safety and draws others to Him, we must have spiritual understanding that is outside the realm of natural understanding, and this requires alert discipline in our daily lives to spend time in The Word and in worship/praise.

By learning to wait upon His presence and move in our lives, we develop a passionate patience and reverent wonder of Him which reflects in our lives as warm friendliness and generous love. All these dimensions fit and grow into each other seamlessly so that each day is a reward in itself for the experience of walking with Jesus. Without this spiritual maturity, it is much like trying the see exactly what is pictured here. You have an idea without clarity. You cannot see the beauty and wonder because you do not have the right focus required. I have glasses but I also had surgery years ago to change my vision. I couldn't see the finer details until the surgery which changed my focus entirely. So that's how I knew I was having trouble seeing because what once was clear started becoming less finite. I can see without my glasses better than most people according to eye doctor but with my lenses, I can really see in fine detail. Once God has opened your eyes to His majesty, the things of this world have an entirely different view. Naysayers may mock and use name calling and misnomers as they cannot see but those who walk in Him, the vision is clear, beautiful and without cloudiness. Whose lenses are you wearing? Are you looking at things?

If we claim that we experience a shared life with him and continue to stumble around in the dark, we're obviously lying through our teeth--we're not living what we claim. But if we walk in the light, God himself being the light, we also experience a shared life with one another, as the sacrificed blood of Jesus, God's Son, purges all our sin.

1 John 1:6-7

Light Living!

Experiences we have and choices we make add or take away from the weight of life's luggage. When stress, tension, challenging times, and pain begin to pile onto you, you gave a choice to pack and carry it or to give it to Jesus. If we pack it away and do not allow Him to work on our behalf, then that weight becomes like a cup put over the light He is in our lives. It becomes a lampshade first then as we continue to dwell in it, it smothers our light cloaking it in pressure and pain. Light living means not only to walk in His Light but to give Him your burdens to share so the weights are reduced.

We will always have burdens, fears and circumstances that challenge our lives but if we let them go into His capable hands, then we can relax in Him. Recently, I went on a trip after my back surgery. I was told I could not lift or pull anything at all, so I arranged to have a chair transport me from gate to gate and my luggage was checked so I didn't have to worry about the weight of it. When we got to our destination, the luggage was picked up by the Porter, put on the wheelchair with me, and carried to the vehicle. The point being I had to give up my independence and rely on someone else to get the release from the weights. If you are like me and you are an independent person, it is hard to let go. I could proclaim my independence and struggle with the weights of all I pack, or I can walk in the freedom of Him. For it is only in the letting go that true freedom is achieved and identity of self is found in Christ Jesus.

Just like my luggage at the airport, I could choose to do it myself but would only end up in a worse place in my health. Interestingly enough, I discovered by just letting go and relying on those who knew...the airport has a lot of shortcuts and behind the scenes that I never would have seen if I had not yielded my independence. Tough times and uncomfortable situations come to everyone. Walking in the light and Living in the light means that you do not do it alone but rather press into The Master and trust His leading. I'm pressing on the upward way. Lord, be my vision, my light in the darkest moments of life. Guide me in perfect peace through the storms of life into your everlasting light.

So if you're serious about living this new resurrection life with Christ, act like it. Pursue the things over which Christ presides. Don't shuffle along, eyes to the ground, absorbed with the things right in front of you. Look up, and be alert to what is going on around christ-that's where the action is. See things from his perspective. Your old life is dead. Your new life, which is your real life -even though invisible to spectators-is with Christ in God. He is your life. When Christ (your real life, remember) shows up again on this earth, you'll show up, too-the real you, the glorious you. Meanwhile, be content with obscurity, like Christ.
Colossians 3:1-4

The Invisible Pursuit!

"Look up and be sweet"...my grandpa's words linger in my head and heart. When he passed from this world, he had just attended the "best prayer meeting ever" according to him and he lied down to sleep and awoke in Heaven. Being serious about a pursuit means you give it your all. You put all that you have in it but in this pursuit, we are chasing the higher calling. which means it is constantly growing within us through our life experiences until the moment we step into eternity. We must change our attitude and perspective to change our altitude. We don't have to be the number one or latest, greatest to accomplish his will.

We only need to lean into Him. It's a place of invisibility or obscurity because when others look at us as we walk in Him, they only see Him. He takes the front seat; all the credit goes where it belongs, and you become His hand extended...a part of the work of Christ. Not the main show, but a piece of what He is doing. Beware showmanship and those who constantly call attention to themselves in His name for He isn't in elevation of man's name but rather the name of The Father God and the Son Jesus...He...is the Spirit of Truth. So don't look at the things around you saying I'll never get what I dream of or my wants/desires here on Earth-that's a shuffling lifestyle, beat down by weights He never intended you to bear. Rather Look Up and Be Sweet! Be alert to what He is doing and what's going on in the spiritual realm. that's where the action is...in Him.

Is anyone crying for help?
God is listening, ready to rescue
you. If your heart is broken, you'll
find God right there; if you're
kicked in the gut, he'll help you
catch your breath. Disciples so
often get into trouble; still,
God is there every time.
He's your bodyguard, shielding
every bone; not even a finger gets
broken.
Psalms 34:17-20

Pot of Gold!

The rainbow sign of promise that God put into place fascinates everyone who sees one. Why? Because of the beauty, uniqueness, and the promise. Someone likely in Ireland where they have plenty of misty rainbows due to the moist air climate started a tale of a leprechaun who has a pot of gold at the end of the rainbow. Songs are written like Somewhere Over the Rainbow...the mystery...the intrigue...while we can man make a rainbow through science with light and water...it cannot hold the same intangible shroud of a naturally occurring one...why?

God's promises. God is faithful and always there even in the midst of the darkest storms of life. God meets us where we are. Think of it this way...the rainbow is there in the storms; it just takes His Sonlight to reflect the goodness through the darkness.
God is listening. God is there. He'll help you catch your breath. God is constant. He's your bodyguard shielding you from the worst life has as He works for you. If you want His best, get your eyes off your circumstances, and begin to worship Him. Worship is like the refractive power in His Sonlight that bends your vision to see the Rainbow of His promises. Look at Him, give Him your best smile and run to Him telling Him everything because He cares for you, and He will work all things out for your best. Open yourself to Him and see how profoundly good He is!

You can easily enough see how this kind of thing works by looking no further than your own body. Your body has many parts limbs, organs, cells-but no matter how many parts you can name, you're still one body. It's exactly the same with Christ. By means of his one Spirit, we all said good-bye to our partial and piecemeal lives. We each used to independently call our own shots, but then we entered into a large and integrated life in which he has the final say in everything. (This is what we proclaimed in word and action when we were baptized.) Each of us is now a part of his resurrection body, refreshed and sustained at one fountain his Spirit where we all come to drink. The old labels we once used to identify ourselves -labels like Jew or Greek, slave or free are no longer useful. We need something larger, more comprehensive. I want you to think about how all this makes you more significant, not less. A body isn't just a single part blown up into something huge. It's all the different-but-similar parts arranged and functioning together. If Foot said, "I'm not elegant like Hand, embellished with rings; I guess I don't belong to this body," would that make it so? If Ear said, "I'm not beautiful like Eye, transparent and expressive; I don't deserve a place on the head," would you want to remove it from the body? If the body was all eye, how could it hear? If all ear, how could it smell? As it is, we see that God has carefully placed each part of the body right where he wanted it.

1 Corinthians 12:12-18

Body functionality!

The photo here is an x-ray of my body, specifically looking at the hardware holding my spine in place. To have a more functional body, I had to say goodbye to some old parts of me and new hardware was introduced but sometimes especially in weather changes, my body doesn't like this decision and fights it sending pain signals to my brain. Our bodies are integrated systems that react to external and internal changes. I mean the awful thing we call cancer isn't a monster but rather our own cells growing out of control taking over our functioning cells. We see this in our culture today as a society where the morals and character of the world are invading the church rather than the church functioning as it should as a body of believers. The truth is if we functioned as we should, this worldly agenda would not progress, but we are too busy trying to grow ourselves in our own way that many become like cancer to the body of Christ. Our purpose is to function together, and this is how Christ is glorified and how we function as He desires.

My body has not functioned as it should for a while now. It will never be the same body as I was born with because there have been many surgeries, illnesses and hardware has been added. My body has been changed. But body functions can adapt to change, newness and roles. As a brain trainer, this excites me because it means that we can change the way we think and learn through training. I go to PT to make my body more functional. This is what God is calling us to do. What part of the body isn't functioning as it should or needs help? Look around you. The people around you are a part of the body or a missing part who need to know. How can you bring more functionality to the body? By reaching out to those in need. Help those hurting, pray for those struggling, read/study and engage others in His high calling to win others to Christ. Each of us is so important. We are not to outgrow others, so we become pompous cancer but rather to dwell and serve so that we become more usable to the kingdom. Struggling with another "Christian" who has done you wrong? Offer forgiveness.

The path forward for functioning is forgiveness. Say it, write it, send it... "I forgive you for hurting me with your actions and I choose to believe despite the appearance to the contrary that you had good intentions towards me. I will pray for you even though you did me wrong because in Christ all things given to Him are made new. I turn you over to His care and judgement in this situation." Then let it go. You may feel like that person is a screw in your spine and trust me I know how that feels. But remember this, through Christ, all things even those intended for evil can become good. Lean in and allow this process of forgiveness to heal you rather than become a cancer of bitterness in your soul and the body of Christ.

I'm not saying that I have this all together, that I have it made. But I am well on my way, reaching out for Christ, who has so wondrously reached out for me. Friends, don't get me wrong: By no means do I count myself an expert in all of this, but I've got my eye on the goal, where God is beckoning us onward-to Jesus. I'm off and running, and I'm not turning back.
Philippians 3:12-14

Eye on The Goal!

When a runner gets off the block on a run, one is told to keep their eyes on the finish line and not be distracted by those around them. Paul is saying exactly this to the church in Philippians. Focus matters! It's not that any of us have it all together. Times are tough for everyone! Everyone I know is struggling in some way with health or finances or in need of wisdom and direction or family matters or kids or. the list is endless. This world is not our goal and when our eyes are focused here, we cannot see the opportunity that God is putting before us through the trials...we only see the dust and here the footsteps of others getting past us or catching up to us.
We are not the end all be all and nothing is this Earth is worth holding onto more than the precious souls that God has given us the opportunity to reach.

The other night I kept hearing banging sounds like a car door opening and closing...Wes went out and it was a coon trying to get into the trash can. He was sitting on the lid of the can and focused so intently on getting into it that he had no idea what was happening around him. His eye was on his goal, but he was getting in his own way. Sometimes we get in our own way and forget that the goal isn't ours alone but rather a goal set before us by God himself to make Heaven our home and to take as many of our fellowman with us as we can. We get so focused on our way or the highway that we refuse to heed advice from those who are on the same path with us encouraging us along. I remember a couple of years ago when we traveled with some friends down a long path to a cave and boy, was that trip back up that path tough! We had to keep encouraging each other along because it was an extremely hard hike and exhausting, but we made it back to the top not under our own strength but because of each other pressing us forward.

Journeys in life don't always take us to places we want to go and sometimes they are fast trips down to the bottom of discouraging situations but through Him we can get back up. Through Christ, we can achieve a glorious experience as we travel back up that mountain by allowing ourselves to join with others...pull them along, let them encourage you and walk together towards the goal. Yes, it is a race...the human race...to the prize, which is the high calling, but this race isn't declaring only one a winner but rather all who arrive. We aren't in a hurry to get there, and no person knows the time that he/she will arrive...we only know that if we keep our eyes on Him-the author and finisher of our faith then and only then will we reach the end.

The world is unprincipled. It's dog-eat-dog out there! The world doesn't fight fair. But we don't live or fight our battles that way never have and never will. The tools of our trade aren't for marketing or manipulation, but they are for demolishing that entire massively corrupt culture. We use our powerful God-tools for smashing warped philosophies, tearing down barriers erected against the truth of God, fitting every loose thought and emotion and impulse into the structure of life shaped by Christ.
Our tools are ready at hand for clearing the ground of every obstruction and building lives of obedience into maturity.
2 Corinthians 10:3-6

Tools of our Trade!

Who are we? What are we? We are tools in the hands of a Mighty God with purpose! Life and the world don't fight fair! But we were designed for a different world...a God world. A tool...that's culturally a negative thing to be called as in a person who doesn't think for themselves, but it used by others...but God called us to be His. In His hands our limited means, our sicknesses, our abilities, and inabilities all become His tools when yielded to Him.

How can I be used of Him? By surrendering all into His hands to be used by Him and trusting that His purpose is above. It isn't a marketing tool or for manipulation but rather for the tearing down of the falseness of this world, demolishing the corrupt culture, smashing warped philosophies, tearing down barriers against the Truth of God....but to do all this...to be used as He desires, we must fit every loose thought, emotion and impulse into the Christ structured life. We must capture the fear and speak peace over it. We must capture the negativity and speak His Truth over it. We must not allow others to mold us by other ways and means. We are to be steadfast and unmovable, always abounding in the work of the Lord. I have watched Wes use his machine to tear down and it is something mighty to watch...the tools are powerful when used by a knowledgeable person. God is omniscient. He knows all of comings and goings. He can do mighty things when we allow Him to use us.

Capture those loose impulses that make you lose your temper and yield that powerful nature to Him. With a person who is complaining and negative, it is hard for God to do anything because they aren't reflecting who He is but rather all of the negative thoughts and emotions built up in frustration of this world. When a person is accepting of who is He and that whatever is sent their way is a piece of the pattern of what He is developing, they can yield even if it means being broken because they understand it takes broken glass to make a stained-glass masterpiece. Lord, today let me be yielded. Not fighting your ways but rather at peace knowing that you have ALL things under your master's hand. Lord, let me be a tool, a piece of pipe or an instrument of grace or whatever you need me to be in this hurting and broken culture! I am your tool! Yielded!

Jesus, overhearing, shot back, "Who needs a doctor: the healthy or the sick? Go figure out what this Scripture means: 'I'm after mercy, not religion.' I'm here to invite outsiders, not coddle insiders." Just then a woman who had hemorrhaged for twelve years slipped in from behind and lightly touched his robe. She was thinking to herself, "If I can just put a finger on his robe, I'll get well." Jesus turned -caught her at it. Then he reassured her: "Courage, daughter. You took a risk of faith, and now you're well." The woman was well from then on. Then Jesus made a circuit of all the towns and villages. He taught in their meeting places, reported kingdom news, and healed their diseased bodies, healed their bruised and hurt lives. When he looked out over the crowds, his heart broke. So confused and aimless they were, like sheep with no shepherd. "What a huge harvest!" he said to his disciples. "How few workers! On your knees and pray for harvest hands!"
Matthew 9:12-13, 20-22, 35-38

The Hem of Faith!

Yesterday when we heard the diagnosis from the doctor, immediately fear tried to enter that place but my mom tranquilly listened. As I watched her, I was desperately clinging to every word of the doctor, but I could see that mom was hearing another. I'm sure her emotions were all over the place but at that moment, she pushed through the crowd of emotions/feelings to stretch out to touch His hem. She was thinking to herself, if I can just touch Him then I will have the strength to walk this journey for the harvest...I know this because as she quietly left the room with my dad, I sat there bombarding the doctor with scenarios and questions. When she returned, she had cloaked herself in peace and she reminded us all of the lives touched through her cancer walk & testimony last time. She said "it is all about the lives we touch, the harvest". To have a testimony, you must first pass through the test.

My mom is a laborer in all things. She is the most energetic and hardest working woman I know. she has lives and walks in the gift of faith which cloaks her in peace. If in one of the darkest moments of her life, she reached out to Him to gather her strength from the touch of His hem...then today can be the days of miracles. When God looks out over the Earth, He sees a huge harvest but only a few laborers. He commands us to get on our knees and pray for harvest hands. Today will you get on your knees and pray urgently and constantly for this precious laborer, Teresa White? Pray for a miracle of mercy and grace. Pray for a miracle of healing. Pray for a harvest of souls touched through the journey no matter what route we must take. Pray for strength and wisdom. Pray for the harvest and this sweet laborer.

Update: Mom is cancer free as God touched her, just as she touched the hem of His Garment!!

So we're not giving up. How could we! Even though on the outside it often looks like things are falling apart on us, on the inside, where God is making new life, , not a day goes by without his unfolding grace. These hard times are small potatoes compared to the coming good times, the lavish celebration prepared for us. There's far more here than meets the eye. The things we see now are here today, gone tomorrow. But the things we can't see now will last forever.
2 Corinthians 4:16-18

Don't Give up! Give it up!

The parable Jesus told of the seed is really on my mind today as I watched seed being sown into lives the last two days. Sowing seed is the planting process, and that seed must go into good soil and then the activation process starts. Many times, it looks like nothing is happening and you feel like giving up as the apostles did in this passage. Appearance is not always reality. Down deep that seed is activated to give up the secret as it falls apart to bring forth new life. The eternal is not what we see now...just as flowers come and go, seasons change, hair grows and falls, wrinkles & aches/pains set it...all these are the outside things that appear as falling apart but on the inside where the secret seed has taken root, new life eternal is growing and what looks like a loss becomes new life. I have to say that sometimes things look impossible or at least appear unlikely but God. The things we invest in now can be eternal or they can be used up and wasted. It's a choice of sowing...where you place the seed matters. You can cast widely with the seed you sow, or you can be targeted and purposeful to grow a good crop. God is purposeful as a good gardener. He sows seed in fertile ground but often for it to become fertile, the tilling and working of the ground must be done. Rocks and sticks and other things that hinder must be removed so that the seed when cast will find good rest.

After the seed takes root, it multiplies and becomes fruitful. There is still growth happening underneath far more than your eyes can see. For the seed becomes more as it multiplies beneath the surface replicating and breaking up the ground. Along our fence line, Wes planted a dead looking piece of bamboo. For years, nothing happened. Other plants grew but the bamboo did not. Then this year suddenly, a huge crop of bamboo appeared lining up across the fence line growing tall and quickly. This is because despite all the years of nothing evident to our eyes, something was happening beneath the ground. The bamboo took root and grew, putting down deep root systems and reproduction was happening. We know from our neighbors' experience that the challenge now is to control the reproductive area because this bamboo is an invasive plant and will try to take over. It grows deep and long and wide under the ground before showing itself. We wanted this hedge but now we must control how far it spreads. Like, we must control what seed it planted and rooted in our lives and that of those around us because not all seed is good, healthy, fruitful, and nourishing.

We must be cautious that we sow to eternity and not to the moment. We must root deep and thoughtfully. We must stay rooted in His grace so we are not led to plant false seeds and invasive species which will seem to be ok now only to spring to life taking over because it took root deep in our lives while we allowed it unawares. Don't give up on the promises of God. Give your life, your seed, your future up to Him to be used and He will multiply and produce for you the future He wills for you, and it will be amazing throughout until eternity.

Arise, shine; For your light has come! And the glory of the Lord is risen upon you. For behold, the darkness shall cover the earth, And deep darkness the people; But the Lord will arise over you, And His glory will be seen upon you. "The sun shall no longer be your light by day, Nor for brightness shall the moon give light to you; But the Lord will be to you an everlasting light, And your God your glory. Your sun shall no longer go down, Nor shall your moon withdraw itself; For the Lord will be your everlasting light, And the days of your mourning shall be ended.

Isaiah 60:1-2, 19-20

My version!

Two different versions of Scripture that say the same thing using a little language difference. This prophecy is for Israel & the bride of Christ. Both start with... Wake up sleepy-head...it's time...God's glory is rising in you and will be seen in you by all. The key is realizing that the light of your days and nights isn't the sun & moon which governs those tied to this planet but rather God is your Sun (the Son) and His reflection of Glory in us is brighter than the moon dispelling the darkness such as there is none in His presence. He is calling His children to Him and The Time of The rapturous taking away is close. He has given us so many signs to know and they are happening all around us. I remember as a youngster thinking God, I want you to come but I also want to experience life, marriage, children...this is a normal earth tied reaction.

When you are in the throes of a good dream, it seems to be reality and when you awaken, it may take a few minutes to clear the cobwebs of the dream and fully awaken. God is waking us gently then shaking us to get us to clear the false reality of earth-bound thinking. We are not limited by this world. This world is not our home. Escape the bonds of limitations and begin to see His glory. Miracles are happening! Revival is shaking...Jesus is coming...if you knew for sure that today was the day, what would you do? Tell someone? Give? Share? Reach out? Why are you waiting? We do not know the day nor the hour, but the signs are everywhere and there's such a feeling in the air that even the blasphemous, deceived devils are screeching and clawing in political arenas thinking as they did at His birth that an earth-bound event is on the horizon. How sad is it that so many are being deceived and lost. Lord, remove the dream cobwebs from my eyes and let me see your glory. Reveal it in me, draw me closer to you so that others may see your light in my life and know you. Work miracles of restoration and healing through me in the lives of others. In the blessed and precious name above all names Jesus Christ! (IS60:1)

Hold fast the pattern of sound words which you have heard from me, in faith and love which are in Christ Jesus. That good thing which was committed to you, keep by the Holy Spirit who dwells in us.
II Timothy 1:13-14

Distortions!

Reflections in water often distort the pattern they are replicating except in the still and quiet...then you get gorgeous beauty that thrills the soul. Paul was exhorting us to the still and quiet by saying Hold Fast...he means don't be shaken and led astray by all these end time fakes. That good thing...salvation...committed to you and kept by the Holy Spirit in you holds you steady in life's winds. Keep the course, hold the pattern...God is coming! Often, we get out lives distorted by the things that we see and perceive to be as the truth when in reality, they are the furthest thing from the truth! Life is full of distortions that confuse us and cause angst. These distortions can cause us to be left feeling lost and abandoned by God, but the reality is God is always there, even when we cannot see Him clearly. Dip your hand into the Living Water and feel the nail scarred hand. Trust in Who He is and What He says is Truth! Do not be misled by the things of the world but trust instead.

"At that same time, a fine vineyard will appear. There's something to sing about! I, God, tend it. I keep it well-watered. I keep careful watch over it so that no one can damage it. I'm not angry. I care. Even if it gives me thistles and thornbushes, I'I just pull them out and burn them up. Let that vine cling to me for safety, let it find a good and whole life with me, let it hold on for a good and whole life."
Isaiah 27:2-5

The clinging vine!

In times of stress, we turn to those/that which is our anchor but often when life seems smooth, we pull the anchor up and drift/move in different directions...sometimes allowing the winds of change around us to blow us into situations or circumstances that we should never have been in had we made sure that the wind in our sails was that of God and not the world. God has cultivated a fine vineyard full of fruitful Christians and He tends us, watering, pruning, and caring so no one can damage the vine. Sometimes we produce things differently than He intended but He prunes those away and burns them up. The job of the vine is to cling to God and His framework for safety so that we can grow, fund a good, whole life and be fruitful. Just like that anchor.... if the vine chooses to unwind and pull away from His support, the little foxes will come and tug, pull and eat the fruit so there is nothing left when the Master comes.

God is careful of you, but you must also choose to lay it down, cling to Him and not allow the wandering. Times are getting harder. Keep your focus on Him. Anchor tightly, cling closely.... the storms will rage but you are in His care. Remember that when the tide comes and pulls, when the wind rages and the vine is shaking around you. Clinging to Him. He is the main Vine; we are the branches. Cling to Him...don't break away in your own way. Trust that He has the perfect plan for you no matter what it looks like.

Jesus was quick to comfort them: "Courage! It's me. Don't be afraid." As soon as he climbed into the boat, the wind died down. They were stunned, shaking their heads, wondering what was going on. They didn't understand what he had done at the supper. None of this had yet penetrated their hearts.
Mark 6:50-52

Heart penetration!

Rest can be a weapon to help you sustain for the storms or journeys ahead. Take Inventory If you are constantly taking inventory of what you don't have, you cannot see what you do have. Change Perspective. Look at things from a different vantage point. Keep Going Forward-Stay in the Boat. Wonderful things can happen in the storms that He sends us because His timing is perfect, and He uses these to build our character and develop us. When you get so focused on the storm, you fail to recognize Jesus for who He is or where He is. He was going to pass them by but stopped when they called out. Recognize His voice in the middle of your storm. The storms stopped as soon as Jesus got in the boat...if you are strong, you often try to prove it. Let Him be the "more than enough" for you by calling out and letting Him into your boat. Wow! That is a super powerful share! Your enough cannot be more than enough unless you step out of the way. Then God spoke....as I looked around the room... And despite all they experienced, none of this had yet penetrated their hearts. It's the YET. Your Experience Test. What will you do with Jesus? Will you allow your heart to be penetrated or will you go thru it repeatedly in order to be the person God wants you to be?

If with heart and soul you're doing good, do you think you can be stopped? Even if you suffer for it, you're still better off. Don't give the opposition a second thought. Through thick and thin, keep your hearts at attention, in adoration before Christ, your Master. Be ready to speak up and tell anyone who asks why you're living the way you are, and always with the utmost courtesy. Keep a clear conscience before God so that when people throw mud at you, none of it will stick. They'll end up realizing that they're the ones who need a bath. It's better to suffer for doing good, if that's what God wants, than to be punished for doing bad.

That's what Christ did definitively: suffered because of others' sins, the Righteous One for the unrighteous ones.He went through it all-was put to death and then made alive to bring us to God.

1 Peter 3:13-18

Mud—slinging contest!

There's a phrase I like called "like water off a duck's back" because it means it just slides away without making any impressions at all. This is how Christ Jesus wants us to live: Without a worldly care. Every day things are going to come at you to make you feel lost and frustrated and overwhelmed but you can look at it as a mud pit to wallow in or take it as just another moment of memories good or bad. At LearningRx, we are constantly teaching our clients YET.

We are not complete in His image YET. As you read what Peter is saying here, you can see that the purpose is understanding that God is your ultimate authority and no matter what happens from flat tires to flat bank accounts, God has the ultimate say so as long as you are heart/soul doing His purpose, forget anything that assails you from negative words to criticisms (unless they are constructive and helpful) to downright mudslinging. I mean they beat Jesus and put Him to death with lies for doing good.... we cannot expect a perfect acceptance of who we are by society because we are different, and we are above the mud. You cannot get someone out of the mud who is slinging it at you by slinging it at them. In fact, if you get down in the mud with them, then you both get dirty and stuck. But if you use the Living Water to wash and help, the mud becomes just dirty water, and that person can rise to the top and get out of the pit. This requires keeping your attention and focus on the right thing though. The struggle is real. It doesn't mean you ignore wrong, but it does mean that you manage yourself as Christ our example did.

Hallelujah! It's a good thing to sing praise to our God; praise is beautiful, praise is fitting. God's the one who rebuilds Jerusalem, who regathers Israel's scattered exiles. He heals the heartbroken and bandages their wounds. He counts the stars and assigns each a name. Our Lord is great, with limitless strength; we'll never comprehend what he knows and does. God puts the fallen on their feet again and pushes the wicked into the ditch. Sing to God a thanksgiving hymn, play music on your instruments to God, Who fills the sky with clouds, preparing rain for the earth, Then turning the mountains green with grass, feeding both cattle and crows. He's not impressed with horsepower; the size of our muscles means little to him. Those who fear God get God's attention; they can depend on his strength.

Psalms 147:1-11

The Word that Works!

I chuckled when I heard my own advice to one person repeated to another as if it were their advice which in fact it now was...because the words had become theirs...they had embraced them. This is the power of The Word.

"The Word was with God and The Word was God and The Word became flesh and dwelt amongst man, but they did not know Him." The Word indicates Jesus but more than that...it indicates the power of The Word that works. In Psalms 147, David now sits on a throne as king, and He realizes the power of a command whether written or spoken by a king or commander to those who choose to embrace the words.
Rebellion is simply choosing not to follow the words whether written or verbal of a person in charge. It is choosing to go one's own way without embracing direction or rules of another and it is dangerous because it leads to destructive behaviors by not learning from those who have been there. Scripture says rebellion is as the sin of witchcraft...both are a total about face from The Word that works in our lives.

But for words to work we must completely embrace them and then they become living and breathing in our lives. A person you respect who states your hairstyle looks nice and cute on you means a little if you respect their opinion and embrace it but if that person also is a hairstylist who owns their own salon and you respect them, their words have more power. I know this from personal experience!

Words have the power that you allow them to have in your life. If someone says something you disagree with, those words have little power and your brain will completely dismiss them unless you respect that person, desire to know more of their opinion, wish to persuade them to your own opinion or they are repeated by another you do respect.
God's word has all power because He is The Word! All nature recognizes His authority and so His commands are obeyed instantly by all who respect His authority.
Grasp this! The God of the whole Universe created you and gave you the ability to choose to recognize His Authority in your life or to Choose your own way. Everything that Has breathe will praise God and bow to Him at the end of times as all will recognize His authority but at this moment you have an immensely powerful choice!

**You realize, don't you,
that you are the temple of God, and God himself is present in vou? No one will get by with
vandalizing God's temple, you can be sure
sacred. God's temple is sacred-and you,
remember, you are the temple.
Dont fool yourself. Don't think
you can be wise merely by being relevant. Be
God's fool-that's the path to true wisdom.
What the world calls smart God calls stupid.
It's written in Scripture, He exposes the
hype of hipsters the Master sees through the
smoke screens of the know-it-alls.
1 Corinthians 3:16-20**

4

Wisdom is Not Relevance!

Yesterday I watched in deep sadness as a young girl walked past my vehicle in "relevance" to society but not to God. I thought how sad that she has violated the temple of her body that God created in order to match the ever-changing fads and demands of a fickle society who will throw her away at the first chance and likely already has by the look of her. In contrast, I saw a lady of elegance laid to rest who had faithfully discharged her duties of raising her children in the fear of God. Her temple of Earthly means had now been vacated for her eternal home but as she was laid in repose, there was beauty in her and in those around her in remembrance.

The Master sees all. You cannot fool Him with hype or proper genuflecting. He sees through all the flesh and sinew to the heart. That's why scripture says that His word is a sword that divides and cuts. His truth stated will hurt. Someone reading this will be offended and not like what is being said but the truth is that God not man makes the rules. No government can say if it is just to kill the innocent in the womb, maim people permanently with forced vaccinations, murder the elderly or terminally sick by refusing vital treatment , lie to get an agenda of lies about genders pushed, steal resources to give to another, destroy others through child trafficking , and cause destruction to His temples by forcing children to learn heinous acts as normal...this is a violation of the laws of the most high and these are the acts of the unforgivable. God will not be mocked. I watch in horror all of this around me and in complete confidence that He is still in control. He told us that lies, deceit and good/bad would be twisted as the end of times comes. He told us to remember and study His ways because they are the ways of the highest. They are the truth, the way, the light that He has laid before us through Christ Jesus.

I chose a beautiful rainbow that God himself cast into the sky because that is a symbol of His promise never to flood the Earth again as He did in the days of Noah. This time, fire from Heaven will fall consuming the Earth. Have you ever wondered why certain areas of this Earth scorch so much and so often. It's not the lies of the liberals of global warming. It's the filth stunning the nostrils of God. When God spoke to me this morning to share this word, I knew that many would not receive it, but the truth is that His elect is preparing for His return. They are not playing in the lies of Sodom/Gomorrah. They remember what is sacred and they do not violate His temple with what is relevant to humankind following a fad. God's ways are not and will never be the fickle ways of society. As Paul wrote this letter to the Corinthians, they were choosing "sides" of man's personality and perspectives. Stop it.

You. Yes, YOU are the temple of GOD! YOU are the dwelling place of the highest God Himself! YOU are sacred to Him! Don't choose the "relevant wisdom" of any man, woman, government but walk in His counsel. The path to true wisdom is by walking sacredly before Him in truth no matter what! No matter who calls you names, unfriends you, lies about you or calls themselves relevant. Truth has become an anchor and a lifeline in a societal world of quicksand that is sucking our children under and choking their lives and eternity into hell.

I have been called old fashioned and out of touch. Some have said I am stuck in tradition or legalism which is the word they use to flick off God's laws as meaningless, but this.... this is a call to repentance. Moms & Dads, Choose you this day whom you will serve. Where will you spend eternity? Where will your children be sacrificed? On an altar of popularly and societal demands or at the feet of a living God who will never fail them? YOU choose! Train up those children in His ways and not the way of social norms. He's coming soon. Being relevant to society is not wisdom, it is folly. Serve your children up on the lies of society and you will doom them to an eternity in hell. YOU are His temple, and no one will get by with vandalizing His temple. Judgement is coming.

Thank God! Call out his Name! Tell the whole world who he is and what he's done! Sing to him! Play songs for him! Broadcast all his wonders! Revel in his holy Name, God-seekers, be jubilant! Study God and his strength, seek his presence day and night; Remember all the wonders he performed, the miracles and judgments that came out of his mouth. Seed of Israel his servant!

Children of Jacob, his first choice! He is God, our God; wherever you go you come on his judgments and decisions He keeps his commitments across thousands of generations, the covenant he commanded, The same one he made with Abraham, the very one he swore to Isaac; He posted it in big block letters to Jacob, this eternal covenant with Israel: "I give you the land of Canaan, this is your inheritance; Even though you're not much to look at, a few straggling strangers."

1 Chronicles 16:8-19

Study & Seek!

Memory recall is a wondrous thing. But you can only remember what you experienced or studied. In Chronicles, which is from the root of Chrono meaning time, we are instructed to Study God and His strength, seek His presence day and night; then remember it!!! All of the instructions prior to this led to the memory. Here is how to Study God and increase your memory: Thank God! Gratitude changes the brain! Call out His name! Saying it aloud helps the memory! Tell the entire world who He is and what He has done! Repeating the works increases memory! Sing to Him! Putting it to music increases memory! Play songs for Him! Broadcast all His wonders! Shouting it brings emotion which helps memory! Revel in His Holy Name! Embracing it helps memory! Be jubilant! Joy increases dopamine which helps memory!

And Mary said, I'm bursting with God-news; I'm dancing the song of my Savior God. God took one good look at me, and look what happened- I'm the most fortunate woman on earth. What God has done for me will never be forgotten, the God whose very name is holy, set apart from all others. His mercy flows in wave after wave on those who are in awe before him. He bared his arm and showed his strength, scattered the bluffing braggarts. He knocked tyrants off their high horses, pulled victims out of the mud. The starving poor sat down to a banquet; the callous rich were left out in the cold. He embraced his chosen child, Israel; he remembered and piled on the mercies, piled them high. It's exactly what he promised, beginning with Abraham and right up to now.
Luke
1:46-55

God's Timing!

When we received the news that my husband's precious grandmother went through the veil to her Heavenly Home last night. I just picture her dancing with her husband in joy right now, so grateful to be past the struggles of this life but she never complained to me. She embraced life as God sent it. I think of God's timing often because it is so different than ours. We get so caught up in the minute details of life that we often forget the minutes that matter until they are gone.

In my reading of Luke today, I am fascinated by the contrast of two people when they receive the news of a coming child. Zechariah was old and had given up his dreams of having a child. He was going through the motions of worship when an angel appeared and gave him a promise but because of his frustration with God's timing, he doubted God's vision and promise. So, he lost out on the ability to share the news with others...as in he couldn't speak at all until John was born! He was a priest...one who daily spent time in worship and led others but he let his disappointment block him from getting in on the joy of the news. God's promise happened just as His angel Gabriel said it would, but Zechariah missed out on getting to fully share in it because he let doubt steal his joy because it wasn't in his timetable. Now, let's look at Mary. God's timing wasn't really great for her either as she wasn't officially married yet-engaged but not married, and boy, was the news unexpected for her too! I imagine she faced some really tough circumstances but look at how she accepts God's timing... with joy! She gets excited and bursting with joy even though I am quite sure others around her were not so happy.

She saw the rainbow on the other side of the storm rather than just the storm. She looked forward to God's promise rather than doubting that He could/would do what He said. She had the same experiences in life with let downs and discouraging things as far as God's timing and she had the same Angel messenger who brought the news. The difference was, she knew. She got her news 6 months after Zechariah. She knew the impossible was possible because she had seen it and she was willing to embrace it. Did she question the angel? Sure...she had some I don't know how moments too, but she embraced God's timing despite her circumstances. God's timing is definitely different than ours. I don't always understand His ways, but I choose to believe. I choose to embrace His ways despite my circumstances because He knows way more than I do, and I have a whole Bible full of examples of His doing the impossible and the improbable on His timetable.
God, I want your mercy to flow in me in wave after wave as I admire who you are! I want to scream with joy and dance with goodness that no matter what my circumstances are, I am the most fortunate woman on Earth because of what you have done for me! Thank you for bringing your light into my life and let me dance in my circumstances no matter the timing because I am yours!

On another note, those of you who have been barren and longing for those rainbow babies...I've been dreaming of some cuties in your laps! God's timing! Will you embrace it with joy or whine that He's not doing it in your time? (warning: Zechariah couldn't speak, and Sarah had a similar experience because of her doubt)! Might be time to claim the promise and wait for His timing!

Hallelujah! Thank God! Pray to him by name! Tell everyone you meet what he has done sing him songs, belt out hymns, translate his wonders into music! Honor his holy name with Hallelujahs, you who seek God. Live a happy life! Keep your eyes open for God, watch for his works; be alert for signs of his presence. Remember the world of wonders he has made, his miracles, and the verdicts he's rendered- O seed of Abraham, his servant, child of Jacob, his chosen.

Psalms
105:1-6

The Verdict is in: Praise the Lord!

I awoke at 3am with praise in my heart and on my lips! The jury of nature around me was singing the news aloud that the verdict was in, and God is good all the time! The locusts and crickets hum His praises, the frogs croak in joyful noises and the nocturnal birds of prey hoot His presence! I went to bed with prayer on my lips and heart for a move of God and awoke with confidence that no matter the trials, He is still in control! Praise the Lord! The psalmist says honor His holy name with song of Hallelujahs you who seek God! It's a choice! We can choose joy through pain as night becomes morning. We can choose to live a happy life even while we are in mourning! We can find Him in all the things around us if we are looking for Him and His works! It is our choice!

The verdict is in! The judges of nations and leaders may fail to quantify His goodness but all of nature...the jury of His creation has rendered the verdict from the highest court of creation that God is good, and His mercies are new every morning! What is a Hallelujah? It is a song of praise! It literally means Praise the Lord! How do we translate God's win into our lives: Thank God constantly! Pray to Him by Name! Testify to His goodness! Sing Him Songs! Write His wonders into music! Honor Him in all you do!

"Why are you so polite with me, always saying 'Yes, sir, and 'That's right, sir, but never doing a thing I tell you? These words I speak to you are not mere additions to your life, homeowner improvements to your standard of living. They are foundation words, words to build a life on. "If you work the words into your life, you are like a smart carpenter who dug deep and laid the foundation of his house on bedrock. When the river burst its banks and crashed against the house, nothing could shake it; it was built to last. But if you just use my words in Bible studies and don't work them into your life, you are like a dumb carpenter who built a house but skipped the foundation. When the swollen river came crashing in, it collapsed like a house of cards. It was a total loss."

Luke 6:46-49

The Foundation!

We have most likely all heard the song about the wise man building his house upon the rocks versus the foolish man in the sand. It's easy to think well I am that wise one but are we really or are we fooling ourselves with the home makeover edition? Yesterday a friend posted a sweet upgrade to the home that she had done for her son, and it was amazing and cosmetic. Get this please. Most of the times in life that we are making changes, it's cosmetic but not foundational. We say the right words, make the right deals and move/shake to make things work but we are not making the life change needed to last.

Changing our foundation or firming it up requires challenging work not just cosmetic changes of furniture and paint. Not the change of our tone and our posts but the change in our heart because out of abundance is where we speak. a cosmetic change is temporary and easily changed again while foundational changes have permanence. I'm a brain trainer so I share this with patients a lot. Cosmetic changes are learning concepts again in a new way. Reading a new devotional or trying something in a new manner but foundational changes often mean removing unhealthy habits and retraining the brain into new learning habits. Growth mindset means we restate things in a more positive manner but for growth mindset to take root, we have to dig up the unpleasant habits and work towards a more substantial change. We must dig deep within ourselves to root out that negative mentality and capture those thoughts every time putting them under the words of Christ's dominion. Notice that Jesus was tempted in the wilderness, but He too captured the thoughts/temptations thrown at Him and restated them with scripture covering them. He took the attack at His foundation and poured the word around it by digging a deep footing a putting the words into the footing with concrete! He repeatedly said The Word says.... if Jesus Christ who is the Son of God used the word to solidify His foundational attacks, He was showing us His example!

The devil, The world, The society, the culture, the media, etc....all attack our foundational principles because if you can break the foundation, the house cannot withstand the storms. But if the foundation is constantly being fortified in The Word, the storms may batter and shake...the cosmetics may even suffer but the house itself will remain firm. When we were growing up, my dad would tell us something and my sister would smile sweetly, give dad a hug, say yes sir and then do exactly what she wanted. I would argue, fight, and end up in trouble and I ended up doing the challenging work. I questioned repeatedly why I couldn't just play it easy and get away with things like she did. I was hardheaded even then. I dug up so much and had to rebuild things so many times because I let the storms batter me, but that foundational building and strengthening has made me so much stronger as an adult. I don't hide from the hard because I know my foundation is strong. I know the greater is He!!!

Life changes come and go. We will experience things we never anticipated, and it will rock our core. It is time to work on digging deep into the bedrock. Fix your foundation with solid concrete of his words. Know that you know for the shaking is coming. The cliffs, mudslides, fires of life, tornadoes, hurricanes, and strong storms are literally all around. Your cosmetics may suffer but if you dig deep and make those footings strong... your foundation will be there. Your house will stand. You will be able to correct the cosmetic damage because the walls will remain.

Therefore when Jesus perceived that they were about to come and take Him by force to make Him king, He departed again to the mountain by Himself alone.

So when they had rowed about three or four miles, they saw Jesus walking on the sea and drawing near the boat; and they were afraid.

But He said to them, "It is I; do not be afraid." Then they willingly received Him into the boat, and immediately the boat was at the land where they were going Jesus answered them and said "Most assuredly, I say to you, you seek Me, not because you saw the signs, but because you" ate of the loaves and were filled. Do not labor for the food which perishes, but for the food which endures to everlasting life, which the Son of Man will give you, because God the Father has set His seal on Him." John 6:15, 19-21, 26-27

Intuition!

Jesus had just performed miracles that impressed the authorities of that day do the "kingmakers" of that political society decided to force him to become "king" or the political head to their decision policies. Things haven't changed. People are the sane fickle bunch now as they were then. They wanted to control the "miracles" and abilities so they could achieve money, power & status. But God himself dwelled in this man's body and He knew them, so He departed to be by himself to rediscover Himself and His humility. He decided to go walk the mountains and the beaches, walk on the water and just be. He needed alone time to realign then when he rejoined them, they were fearful thinking he was a ghost, but He announced himself, so He was recognized and got into the boat. Immediately they arrived at shore meaning they were almost there before He joined. Then the people clamor once again for demonstrations of His power not because they believe Him or even trust Him but because their bellies are filled with man's food and a desire for power. It is so easy to get caught up in the fame/fortune cycle. The desire to be known is human nature at its worst. We are so shallow. Legacy....it's a desire to leave behind us a name that holds something...power, fame, fortune, heritage...more... and yet...who am I?

We as humans set our minds on laboring to meet our needs rather than laboring for God and allowing Him to meet our needs. Jesus taught this through the provision of food for four thousand from a little bread then again feeding five thousand with just a couple of minnows and rolls but still the people missed it. He very plainly tells us through scripture over and over to work for Him and allow Him to be our provider but yet we labor over and over to provide for ourselves missing or choosing to ignore His message of faith. He desires us to labor for eternal food-everlasting life.... reaching those who are perishing and allow the daily bread to be taken care of by Him, but we are so lacking in our trust. We fail to realize that the stamp of approval, the seal God has set isn't on that which fades and is consumed easily but is on the meat that requires rendering and marinating through His Spirit. Recently when there was a baby formula shortage, panic ensued because so many worried how they would feed their kids.... this is only a small example of how devastating it will be in end times when food shortages are rampant, and people are fighting over an old can of food because they are desperate to provide for the physical. If we can grasp this....it is so much more important now to feed the spiritual man than the physical. The spiritual man who is well fed/watered will never truly hunger/thirst physically because of God's Providence.

Think of Elijah in the desert provided for by ravens. God knows your need. If you are struggling for a physical need, perhaps it is a spiritual awakening that is needed. Yes. Yes. Yes. Lord, we hear you. We know that our vision needs to be cast away from the carnal into the eternal and we must get our eyes off our physical limitations and begin to see what can be wrought in the spiritual. Help us Lord to see what you are doing. Help us to trust where you are leading even though the waters may look murky. Help us to trust you to know best.

As they were leaving Jericho, a huge crowd followed. Suddenly they came upon two blind men sitting alongside the road. When they heard it was Jesus passing, they cried out, "Master, have mercy on us! Mercy, Son of David!" The crowd tried to hush them up, but they got all the louder, crying, "Master, have mercy on us! Mercy, Son of David!" Jesus stopped and called over, "What do you want from me?" They said, "Master, we want our eyes opened. We want to see!" Deeply moved, Jesus touched their eyes. They had their sight back that very instant, and joined the procession.
Matthew 20:29-34

What do you want from me?

I have noticed in life that we usually want what we don't have and many times we don't want what we already have. This is our conundrum. It looks fine and deserving, exciting and wonderful from another's point of view but once it's ours, the new wears off and we are left with less than we desired. Jesus is deeply moved by our hurting hearts. He knows our pain and heartaches like no other and his compassion is a deeper well than any I know.

As Jesus and his followers were departing the city, they passed by two beggars who were blind. The beggars knew there was a commotion because they could hear it and when they found out it was Jesus passing their way, they cried out. But for what did they cry?

They cried for Mercy! Not money, not gifts, not more of Earthly goods but Mercy! Obviously, they were pretty loud because it says the crowd tried to get them to hush but that made them louder. They cried loud and long enough that Jesus stopped and called over to them. The size of the crowd must have prevented Jesus seeing them and their plight, but He heard them. He heard the cry for Mercy! They had the attention of the Savior. He had stopped. He was tuned into them, and He asked..."What do you want from me?" They didn't describe their plight. They didn't whine or complain. They didn't bemoan their situation. They said, "we want to see"..."we want our eyes opened". Stop a minute here with me.

We are blind beggars in a world of troubles. We always have need. These blind beggars could have asked for wealth, wisdom, fame, or any number of things but Mercy rewrote their life because they asked for vision. Proverbs 29:18 is wisdom from God given through Solomon in which he states that lack of vision causes people to perish.

Vision is not just a physical experience. Vision is a state of heart and mind. Vision is an important sense, but it is also a necessary thinking skill. Vision allows for hope and allows a future. The verse says here that Jesus was Deeply Moved. We know He physically approached them at this point because it then says He touched their eyes, and they got their sight back that very instant. I don't know what caused their blindness nor how long they had been blind. All I know is that they cried loudly and constantly for Mercy. I know they would not be hushed even though others around them including family and friends, important people and crowds tried to quiet them. I know they hungered for Mercy and desired vision. As with many stories, the Bible doesn't record what happened next in their lives....it just recorded the moment that Mercy changed their circumstances. Their lives were hard as beggars we assume but we don't know. We only know that they cried out for Mercy and God's mercy rewrote their lives and we know they joined the procession when they gained vision.

Jesus is deeply moved by you. You may feel like the crowd is trying to shut you up...get louder! You may feel hopeless and frustrated, disappointed, and let down. You may feel like a beggar left with crumbs but that's when it us time to get louder! Shout! Scream! Cry! Sing! Jump! Reach for Mercy! The Master stops for Mercy and mercy rewrites lives! There is no point where it is too late! Jesus is asking you...."what do you want from me?" He has given His very life in mercy for your soul. He has prepared a place for you in Heaven. He is ready to give you vision. Are you wandering? Wondering what is next for you in life? Ask Him to open your eyes so you might see Him! Lord, give me vision to see so others may not perish! Master, we want our eyes opened so we might see what it is you have for us to do.

But how can people call for help if they don't know who to trust? And how can they know who to trust if they haven't heard of the One who can be trusted? And how can they hear if nobody tells them? And how is anyone going to tell them, unless someone is sent to do it? That's why Scripture exclaims, A sight to take your breath away! Grand processions of people telling all the good things of God! But not everybody is ready for this, ready to see and hear and act. Isaiah asked what we all ask at one time or another: "Does anyone care, God? Is anyone listening and believing a word of it?" The point is: Before you trust, you have to listen. But unless Christ's Word is preached, there's nothing to listen to.
Romans 10:14-17

Superfluous or Supercilious

How can you trust when truth is quicksand ever changing and unfixed? We live in a time when reality is both too much and too little. We receive information at the drop of a keystroke but strike again and that information has changed to the complete opposite. It's shaky ground, covered in quicksand. How can someone cry out for help if they are unsure if they'll receive help or harm? How can they know who to trust when so much falsehood abounds, and they've never met the real one?

Wes picked a watermelon that had all the signs of readiness and was even a little overripe in appearance, but it had absolutely zero flavor. It wasn't ready. It appeared to be ready, but it wasn't. Paul is repeating Isaiah's questions here in Romans. Am I going about wasting my time? Does anyone care? Are they listening? Trust comes from doing and doing comes from hearing. You have to listen to the voice of God before you act but if no one is going about proclaiming His truth then how will anyone know? No one adores "know it alls". Superfluous information that is unnecessary is wasteful and supercilious people abound in this. The talking heads who say they know but yet their life is no better than others. It's irritating and frustrating that God's word tells us He has given us all power on Earth and in Heaven but acting in His authority sometimes flops and makes us look foolish. How can our test ever become a testimony if we constantly fail at it? Or We never or rarely get credit or results in the areas we pray. What's the point then?

When my boys were small, they had a playroom with shelves and tubs for all of their belongings. I always made them put things up exactly where they belonged with no shortcuts. This frustrated Gabe. He said why does it matter? We are just going to get them all out again soon. And he was right to an extent. That room would get cluttered and cleaned many times a day to his complete consternation. But there was purpose happening called training up a child. They both learned that everything has a place and a purpose. They learned value for this in life as it helped their brains to understand organizational patterns and categorization which are necessary underlying thinking skills for reading and math. They learned because I insisted and through this, they learned trust in methods, systems and that there truly is a place for everyone.

As a teacher, I learned that the best way to check a student for mastery was to have them teach it to another. People learn to trust you because you trust Him and tell them. Tell them the good and the bad. God doesn't fail me. I may get disappointed in His ways or discouraged because the path is foggy but if I keep following the path, I'll see the Living Water flowing. I'll see it in the lives around me. It'll be posted wherever I go eve an obituary. The living water is there, and it never stops. Are you leading others on the path to the falls stumbling often but still getting up and going or have you given the journey up? Your faith may take a hit. You might bomb the test. But you know what.no matter what the grade...you still have a testimony once that test is past. Learn from that one. Pick yourself up. Dust off those heavy guilts, lift up those Holy hands and move forward on the path with head held high. Because unless you tell your testing to others, they'll never know, and it is through the dirt of your failures and flaws that people can see the REAL truth they can trust!

Who has done such mighty deeds, summoning each new generation from the beginning of time? It is I, the Lord, the First and the Last. I alone am he." Don't be afraid, for I am with you. Don't be discouraged, for I am your God. I will strengthen you and help you. I will hold you up with my victorious right hand. For I hold you by your right hand- I, the Lord your God. And I say to you, 'Don't be afraid. I am here to help you. I am doing this so all who see this miracle will understand what it means- that it is the Lord who has done this, the Holy One of Israel who created it.
Isaiah 41:4, 10, 13, 20

Disenquoyment!

Dis-disrespect, En-a measure of type, Quoy-wasteland Ment-noun =A measured wasteland of disrespect I have been awake for hours conversing with God about this untoward generation. A generation who has had an unmatched hunger for something they know not what of but have continued to fill this void with whatever fancy comes their way. The summoning they fill is God, but they have failed to recognize Him as this fulfillment because the bride has lacked the luster to say yes to her bridegroom. She has said yes to the feast as long as it meets her specifications...she has said yes to the dress because it showcases her as important and mighty...she has said yes to the guests because she desires fame/fortune, but she has yet to say yes to the bridegroom because that means commitment to one and only. Instead, she is filled with disenquoyment. I know. It's not a word you can look up. I tried. It's a word God gave me this morning.

I watch SharkTank because it fascinates me with all the gadgets that people create and turn into businesses but also because it fascinates me to see and hear the yearning/searching for fulfillment from those who want fame/fortune to fulfill this wasteland within them and they search for this fulfillment through this measured wasteland of others who are slogging through the same place. The search for fulfillment is palpable. They want so badly to escape the measured wasteland of disrespect (disenquoyment) but yet they seek the escape by drawing from others who sit in the same muck holding onto to more of it...trying to fulfill this insatiable need by giving away wealth to find a sense of belonging, a sense of fulfillment and never achieving it. The summoning comes from God himself and only He can fulfill it.

I awoke with a sense of urgency and a clear awakening to a shift in the balance of power in our world today. The world quakes as the unseen eternal forces size up with a knowing that the trump of God is soon to sound. The calling forth of the last days has begun as spoken of in Joel and referenced in Acts. Greater things He has done, and Greater things are still to come. The church, the true bride who has kept her wicks trimmed and her oil filled is being called to shine her light into a darkened society beckoning as a lighthouse on a hillside. God has empowered her for she has chosen her bridegroom and He picked her dress and He set the feast because He chose her before the foundations of the world were laid.

Miracles, signs, wonders in the Heavens and things beyond our wildest dreams are about to unfold. The true Bride has not wavered. She is unaffected and unattainable by any but her beloved. She is unafraid because her bridegroom comes as the first and the last. He holds her by her right-hand doing miracles for her, through her and because of her. She understands His purpose and yields completely to His leading. God, our bridegroom does these miracles so ALL will understand what it means. So, ALL will know who has done this. So, ALL who feel the summons will know who has called. We live and abide in disenquoyment because we do not recognize His voice. This veritable wasteland of disrespectful conversation and action has come because the bride of Christ chose to say yes to a dress rather than to the bridegroom. It is a wakeup call to recognize and hearken for the hour grows late. The feast is prepared. The garment is ready. The bridegroom comes. What are you waiting on?

For when I tried to keep the law, it condemned me. So I died to the law - I stopped trying to meet all its requirements - so that I might live for God. My old self has been crucified with Christ. It is no longer I who dive, but Christ lives in me. so flive in this earthly body by trusting in the son of God, who loved me and gave himself for me. I do not treat the grace of God as meaningless. For if keeping the law could make us right with God, then there was no need for Christ to die.
Galatians 2:19-21

Yet I live!

Today is a day of much angst in many lives. The law with its ins and outs has achieved remarkable things for the innocent but disappointed those who fight for "rights". The law in and of itself is flawed and no one lives exactly to the law especially to the law of God. For we are human. When a child is born, the child knows only to demand for its own needs to be met but over time and with training learns rules, schedules and timelines that begin to dictate life. This is why Christ tells us to come to Him as a child with no preconceived notions of who He is or what He is capable of because a child's expectations are unlimited by the disappointments and "laws" of life. The faith of a child easily accepts that life can return to a lifeless body without question because that child has no experience with the "laws" of death. The child doesn't understand the boundaries between this life and the next because the child has recently crossed those boundaries into life through Christ.

Life as we know it is finite and defined or bound by the breath in this corpse or being rather than being defined by Christ. My spirit hurts when one I love crosses from this life into the other because I am limited by time/space. I cannot see them or hold them nor embrace their corporeal body so that hurts me and grieves me but the last few mornings, I have awoken with visions of His infinite love and His ultimate purpose in my mind. I have seen loved ones who live embracing on another plane and visions of babies held in several mothers' arms whose children are not currently here on this plane. My mind/spirit/soul has witnessed the crossing of the plane and the boundaries of this "law" of death is no longer a fear or even a circumstance but rather a step in a journey. Wes & I spoke yesterday of the beauty of falling asleep in this life and awakening in another. My grandfather passed in this manner...literally went from one prayer meeting to a celebration party in Heaven. Our finite minds try to bind us to this world and see miracles as being a circumstance of life kept here to this earth when it is the exact opposite. Life with Christ is Life abundance. I do completely believe in miracles happening in this earthly realm. This is why Jesus wept just before calling Lazarus from the grave. He felt the emotional boundaries of the laws of earthly life and yet He knew he transcended that. He wept. Then He wiped his tears and called forth from the grave. The veil between this life and the next was rigidly fixed before Christ but was torn apart in an instant and forever by His resurrection. Get this. Mourning is but a season of life and mostly because we no longer have immediate access to the presence of the one, we love but Christ made this all outdated. Our bodies age and wear because of the "laws" of earth such as gravity. Most of these laws we do not understand but what we must grasp above all of this is we as God's children and His anointed are not bound by the laws of Earth. We operate within them, but we too have the power to call forth life from death and we too transcend the laws of death to live eternally. While some today mourn the loss of many and others mourn the loss of life as they know it, we should be celebrating life. Understanding that for me to live on this Earth is but a means and opportunity to share His limitless grace with others whilst here because our true calling is to reign with Him in eternity. A passing from life to death is no longer. Rather a passing from life on Earth to Life eternal. Which means, there is a choice. Where will Life eternal be spent? A life with Christ walking on a different plane or a life of damnation walking in darkness with weeping and gnashing of teeth for those who are lost and cannot find their way to the place they seek. I cannot imagine a worse fate than being eternally lost in darkness.

Recently I took my staff and went into a cave on a tour and at one point the guide turned off all the lights. That darkness and wandering would drive a mind crazy. This is the darkness that many minds of people here on Earth suffer because God has separated from them already and given them over to depravity. Their minds are lost forever. We remark on the look of lostness, but it is nothing like the true darkness they will wander in for eternity. But Grace. God's Grace, grace that's greater than all our sins. Grace still exists for us. It is still within our grasp to let go of the finiteness of our own minds and embrace His eternal purpose. Let go of your boundaries. Let go of your limits. Come as a child believing. Life....life abundantly still flows and miracles still happen! Today is the day that God is calling you forth from the grave of Earthly life into an eternity with Him. You may walk here 10 more minutes or 10 more years but today He is calling you into Life eternal. Will you hear Him? Donesa, come forth. Come from the grave of earthly dwelling of purpose in Life. Walk into a fullness of Life. Walk into God's fullness where the veil between the planes no longer exists. Walk into His presence. Cross the great divide...for He is the bridge across., the cross bridged the great divide...enter into His salvation.

So be content with who you are, and don't put on airs. God's strong hand is on you; he'll promote you at the right time. Live carefree before God; he is most careful with you. Keep a cool head. Stay alert. The Devil is poised to pounce, and would like nothing better than to catch you napping. Keep your guard up. You're not the only ones plunged into these hard times. It's the same with Christians all over the world. So keep a firm grip on the faith. The suffering won't last forever. It won't be long before this generous God who has great plans for us in Christ-eternal and glorious plans they are! - will have you put together and on your feet for good. He gets the last word;
yes, He does.
1 Peter 5:6-11

Behind the curtain!

When I was a young one, a musical came out called The Wizard of Oz and while some thought it was a fantasy story, it was really a lesson on contentment. No one in the story was happy with who they were and is a tornado changed their lives taking Dorothy on a magical journey of discovery resulting in her learning and teaching others to find contentment with who they are in order to achieve happiness. We live in a world torrid with worries and cares so that our minds & bodies have little rest and much stress which wears us down further. In the Wizard of Oz, everyone was looking to the man behind the curtain to solve their problems when in reality, he had more problems than they did. This is the story of our world. The more we look to man's solutions, the more they will fail us. For we are not made of earthen clay without a purpose; He made us of dust so we could realize that to dust these mortal bodies will return but to Him and with Him we reside.

If you are not shouting right now, then you missed that curve ball. God didn't make you for this earth. He didn't form you for only a whisper of time but for all eternity. He is most careful with you. Watching a potter carefully construct an earthenware vessel or one of glass is awe inspiring because from nothing but dust/sand, a priceless piece of beauty and purpose is born but the process is hot, laborious, time consuming and intense. The glassmaker blows and turns, clips and prods, spins, and stills to form the perfect arch needed to serve the purpose of the maker. Then, the glassmaker carefully with precision puts the art in a place of beauty and light until it is time for usage so that it may fully become the desired vessel chosen. This artist is most careful with this piece as it is a unique one-of-a-kind prized possession with purpose. But only the creator knows its full purpose and how it may be used. Others who look may see a tin man with no heart or a cowardly lion who longs to be more. The point is to trust the process. Live carefree not rent free or carelessly but carefree before God knowing that He has express purpose for your life that is unique like no other. Only you have the gifts, abilities, drive, and personality to accomplish the tasks He has for you. Your time may not even come until you follow that yellow brick road fighting off evil and learning good or your time may come while you are on that road searching for answers but be assured that your time will come and not just once. The creator in His divine way purposes you to be used in many ways and many purposes as long as you are an open vessel to His purposes. I have a beautiful glass dish that sits beside my tub to hold a bar of soap. But that is not it's only purpose nor its original intended purpose for I was careless, and I broke the other half to the beautiful glass heart many years ago. Originally it was given as a beautiful piece to sit on my dresser and hold nothings or somethings but today it holds my rings as I bathe, my memories as I look at it and my bar of soap that cleans me.

Today you may feel broken, without hope or purpose. Disappointed because things of life did not occur as you had dreamed or desired but know this, no matter what part of the road you are on, The Creator who knew you in your mother's womb and knit you together has many purposes for you and your life. You are His, called by name, chosen by design, and created with purpose. He gets the last word. Not a court, a congress, a king, or any other authority is higher than His. God's hand is on you and at the right time, your fullness will be known. Until then, take care. Be watchful and alert. Keep a cool head and a humble heart. The devil would love to derail you. He can't you know unless you choose to allow it. He has no authority except what God allows and you allow. Suffering in any situation is temporary and the results after are almost always a thing of precious beauty. I remember childbirth and the terrible pain but oh the joy of that baby...those sleepless nights, those temps & temper tantrums...wait, I digress...the joy.... Hod has great and glorious plans for you to put you solidly on your feet for good! Remember His great love and care for you. Hold on for Joy is on its way!

Make a joyful shout to the Lord, all you lands! Serve the Lord with gladness; Come before His presence with singing. Know that the Lord, He is God; It is He who has made us, and not we ourselves; We are His people and the sheep of His pasture. Enter into His gates with thanksgiving, And into His courts with praise. Be thankful to Him, and bless His name.
For the Lord is good; His mercy is everlasting, And His truth endures to all generations.
Psalms 100:1-5

The Password!

Knowing the right directions is important to get to a destination but that is only part of the journey. You cannot arrive to the portal of entry to anything from a website to a tourist site without the proper identification that says you belong or the password for entry. Lots of people spend their lives hacking their ways into the lives of others virtually and in person trying to belong but never realizing that God's love makes the entry automatic.

Today I am a little melancholy because I want to be where I cannot, and I regret not making more effort when I had the time. I want to be with my family as the portals of Heaven open, but it is not yet my time. I want to be able to be past this pain and sickness so I can worship fully with my hands raised but my back won't support that right now. I want to be a lot of things to a lot of people that I cannot. I awoke this morning in tears of pain and anguish for all of this with a very heavy heart but that is not where God left me. He gave me a song. He gave me a calling. He reminded me of His love, His endurance through all the generations. He reminded me that no matter where my physical body might be, I can be in His presence, and I can enter His gates. I don't have to wait for a certain time or place to open but I can enter with the password of Holy praise into His Holy of Holies. There I can kneel and make all my petitions know. Although I can just me, not anyone special, I get VIP treatment because I am His. Both of these pictures took place at the exact same moment in time just as God's word over them is the same and yet the perspective of the picture shows a different reflection just as the verse has a slightly different translation. Both show the same & say the same yet show differently and say differently. Nuances of life take us in different directions and sometimes we grow so far apart and yet His love is the string on the kits holding is bound to Him, allowing us to sail in the winds through the difficulties but constantly guiding us through the obstacles. When we get trapped or caught in the branches of life, he disentangles us. I have a song I have been writing for years on this as He has brought me through these places.

This song of praise is my password to eternity. When God opens the portals of Heaven for entry to His beloved, each of us enters with our own unique song of prayer/praise/worship for He gave us a new language unbeknownst to any other. If your heart is heavy and you feel adrift, tug on the string, He's still there guiding...you may be feeling like the winds of life have driven you into a dive or even ensnared you in a mess but I promise you, He's still there working at your snafus, disentangling your messes and giving you winds and wings of love to soar again. Can you hear it? Softly and tenderly, Jesus is calling...enter your password and move into His presence.

Now when Jesus had entered Capernaum, a centurion came to Him, pleading with Him, saying, "Lord, my servant is lying at home paralyzed, dreadfully tormented." And Jesus said to him, " will come and heal him." The centurion answered and said, "Lord, I am not worthy that You should come under my roof. But only speak a word, and my servant will be healed. For I also am a man under authority, having soldiers under me. And I say to this one, 'Go,' and he goes; and to another, 'Come,' and he comes; and to my servant, 'Do this,' and he does it." When Jesus heard it, He marveled, and said to those who followed, "Assuredly, I say to you, I have not found such great faith, not even in Israel! And I say to you that many will come from east and west, and sit down with Abraham, Isaac, and Jacob in the kingdom of heaven. But the sons of the kingdom will be cast out into outer darkness. There will be weeping and gnashing of teeth." Then Jesus said to the centurion, "Go your way; and as you have believed, so let it be done for you." And his servant was healed that same hour.
Matthew 8:5-13

Keep Asking, Seeking & Knocking!

Persistence is a skill because it takes balance to know when to push forward in certain directions and when to take time out. In Matthew 8, Jesus has just given instructions to the disciples on persistence when He is confronted with a level of faith that surprises Him enough to remark on it. The commander has a sick servant, and he asks Jesus to heal him. Jesus says, sure, I'll head that way and the commander says no need, just say the words and it'll be done. This commander recognized the authority Christ had in dominion over all and His faith in Christ & His dominion healed his servant. Jesus remarks that many of his loyal followers will miss out and go to hell while others afar off are saved because of this type of faith. Yesterday, someone asked me whose report did I believe, in response to several needs of healing and intervention in my close family/friends And myself. Attacks both physically, spiritually, emotionally, and financially are ever present around but the devil realizes that his time is super short so more rampant attacks are happening all around. The gloves are off so to speak on his side, but Christians have yet to step up because we are still waiting on the sidelines. Persistence isn't about being annoying to get our way but rather constantly asking, seeking & knocking at the door of God's divinity to be our source. Faith is the substance of things hoped for and the evidence of things not seen. If you hope for something but never voice it, how can it happen. If you desire for something but never act, how can it begin. The practice of faith is like recognizing a lightning strike and knowing it means a storm is coming. I remember counting the seconds between the thunder/lightning when I was a kid to know how close the storm was and the feeling of anticipation as it approached.

So back to the question...whose report do I believe? Gods of course. I do not understand all His ways or timing but like the centurion commander, I recognize His authority and dominion. My issue is I get earth bound rather than realizing that my Lord isn't bound by time nor space. He isn't bound by man's opinions nor timetables. He isn't bound by the limitations we give. He isn't bound by medical science nor by my own bodily limitations. The question then really becomes dominion. I ask unwaveringly, I seek His ways and my options within my current abilities/reach as He has given me this authority to command sickness/disease and other issues to be under my feet, then I begin knocking at the opportunities and possibilities until the door is clearly opened for me. Paul said to not grow anxious or weary in this for in time we will reap. It's hard when you are struggling with progressive or chronic diseases such as degeneration and cancer. These are not fun. They are exhausting and wearing on everything and everyone around you. But there is a key in this-not a formula mind you as I don't believe in those. ASK. Acronym. Ask & it's given (As Sincerely Kneaded: work, press in, push through)
Seek & you'll find (Sew Each Element: everyone, everything, every place Knows when you find -the testimony)
Knock & it will open (Know No One Can Know where/when the door is opened)

Jesus answers...after the centurion ASKed (asked, seeked, knocked) ..."Go, for as you believed so let it be done." So, if my healing is not in this plane of earth, does it mean it is incomplete? Absolutely not and it's not a lack of faith but rather an ACT of faith. Persistence. Keep the ASK! Trust the Authority! Doubt stand in the way of belief and lack of belief inactivates Faith. ASK then Go! I know not the path before me but I'm sure my Savior does for He has walked this road before and knows each bend/curve. All I must do is trust. Persistence...are we there yet Father God? Have we reached the place you want us to be? ASK in peace knowing whose authority is answering!

If you reason with an arrogant cynic, you'll get slapped in the face; confront bad behavior and get a kick in the shins. So don't waste your time on a scoffer; all you'll get for your pains is abuse. But if you correct those who care about life, that's different_-they'll love you for it! Save your breath for the wise they'll be wiser for it; tell good people what you know--they'll profit from it. Skilled living gets its start in the Fear-of-God, insight into life from knowing a Holy God. It's through me, Lady Wisdom, that your life deepens, and the years of your life ripen. Live wisely and wisdom will permeate your life; mock life and life will mock you.
Proverbs 9:7-12

The Choice!

God gave King Solomon infinite wealth & wisdom when he asked for wisdom. He learned young that there was a choice, and he tells the story of travelers walking down a road being beckoned by two different ladies. One is a woman called Lady Wisdom who has prepared a table of sustenance and if openly telling what is available on the menu of life while the other is a prostitute offering secrets and hidden agenda. The choice belongs to each traveler as to where he will decide to reside. But even in the case of a man of wisdom like Solomon, he speaks from a place of knowledge because he too made the mistake more than once of choosing wrongly. We all do. It's human nature but that's just the reason-my dad said an excuse is the skin of a reason stuffed with a lie. The truth is we must own our choices and sometimes those choices own us later in life. Sometimes we pay the price of folly years after we gained the substance of wisdom. I can say that many of my back issues likely come from my youth when I abused my back with things like skydiving and bungie-jumping. At the time, it was just fun with no thought for the future. I look at many who make decisions now and I think, how can you make that decision not knowing how it will affect you later especially with all the controversies surrounding it but then I see...they are young travelers walking along the "Bourbon" Street of life listening to all who call and beckon. The noise of the call is loud, and some take many visits to those thrills of life before they heed the call from Lady Wisdom...and some never hear her voice. Some stop by for a site seeing visit but although the food looks tasty and will give endurance, it takes too long to sit and eat to learn so they swiftly walk through picking up only a crumb or two to nibble while they continue the path into the other ways never understanding there are consequences with deep ramifications that will follow into their grandchildren...

I do not claim to know it all, but I am a student of life. I read, I learn, I listen, and I ponder. Taking time to invest soundly into what will hold and last is more intelligent than throwing money away in a moment on a pleasure that will have no return except when sound investing can be that memory or moment learned. When you make a foolish choice and learn from it, that investment was not a complete waste as learning happened. The church decided somewhere along the way to disguise itself under entertainment instead of plainly sharing the wisdom God gives. The choice for our young became murkier then. The standards are not clearly demarked but rather hidden behind subtle language and games. This trickery is not of God and not a show of wisdom but rather a deceit.

In school we ready a story called The Lady or The Tiger? which is saying we all have choice. In the story, a man must choose between two doors for daring to love the princess. Because of the king's displeasure, two doors or s choice was provided. Behind one was a fierce tiger which would tear him apart in front of the princess and behind the other was a beautiful maiden whom he would be forced to marry. The man looked to the princess because he loved her, and she knew & could see what was behind the doors. She had to choose to save him or kill him and he had to choose to tryst her to save him or kill him. There is no ending to the story for it is left for you to decide. God's love tells us a different story. He didn't leave us with just two doors. He took the door of death for us and left us a door of life. We know which is the door of death by His words and His life. As long as we wander down this road of life listening to the voices harking their wares, we fail to notice that the door to Life has already been opened. Death lost its sting. It has no power. We hold so tightly to our endless wandering and wondering that we fail to see the truth. Live every moment in Him, through Him and for Him. Take your photos and enjoy your life but remember the choice has been made, you have only to choose to follow. Let life deepen into the things eternal that matter and stop wasting days/times on those things which have no substance. Read Proverbs 9. Are you hungry and thirsty for things of God? Take time to taste and see that He is good.

The ways , right-living people glow with light; the longer they live, the brighter they shine. But the road of wrongdoing gets darker and darker- travelers can't see a thing; they fall flat on their faces. Dear friend, listen well to my words; tune your ears to my voice. Keep my message in plain view at all times. Concentrate! Learn it by heart! Those who discover these words live, really live; body and soul, they're bursting with health.

Proverbs 4:18-22

The Right Glow!

The yard is dark tonight except right under the moon. That path I can see for it reflects real soon. My heart hurts now for words I heard were not the ones I wanted. They told a story of a life whose pathway of dark is haunted. The traveler couldn't see his path because he chose the wrong reflection. He turned his eyes from the Maker into the wrong direction. His ears tuned out the true words he heard as he set out on a twisted path converged. Concentrate! Listen! Hear the truth! For this there is living proof! Tune your ears! Hear the message plain! There is but one thing-your life to gain!

The ways of the right glow with life. Reflected from the one true light. The longer they live, the brighter they glow. This is how their path you'll know to follow. The reflection they leave, the words that shine, are not words of theirs nor of mine. Their path runs straight away from the dark so travelers can see and not depart. They don't fall down when shocking news they receive because their reflection is one of peace. The glow they follow is not of the stars for those often burn out and become pieces of char. The light of their glow is true reflection for they are following God's direction. If you get lost and are not sure which path, look to His light for it will hold you fast. His Son's reflection is the pure white light which formed a rainbow in dead of night. This rainbow is a promise not an empty false trail but one that formed from the blood-stripes that fell. From the cross where Christ laid his own life down so that one day you could wear a crown.

Don't let city lights of fortune and fame steal the true light away from His name. His light is true, it is the one glow that still is shining when all else is below. As the first ray of light breaks away from His dawn, He is alive when all else is con. Keep this message in plain view, listen to the words I'm telling you. Jesus is coming again real soon. His reflection is breaking away from the moon. His light stands alone like no other better than any friend or brother. Cling to His light whose reflection you see. For He is the answer for you and for me.

Hallelujah! You who serve God, praise God!
Just to speak his name is praise!
Just to remember God is a blessing-
now and tomorrow and always. From east to
west, from dawn to dusk, keep lifting all your
praises to God! God is higher than anything and
anyone, outshining everything you can see in
the skies. Who can compare with God, our God,
so majestically enthroned, Surveying his
magnificent heavens and earth?
He picks up the poor from out of the
dirt, rescues the forgotten who've been thrown
out with the trash, Seats them among the
honored guests, a place of honor among the
brightest and best. He gives childless couples a
family, gives them joy as the parents of
children. Hallelujah!
Psalms 113:1-9

The Blessing: To Remember Who He Is!

What if today is your day to remember nothing else than who He is? The blessing is to remember who God is. A sunflower is a sunflower, but it remembers who God is. It chases God across the sky by day and drops its head in prayer by night. At the end of its days, it drops its seeds into the ground trusting who God is to replicate itself through the cycle of nature. It doesn't worry about tomorrow but rather lives each day to remember who God is because that is the blessing. Hallelujah! Just speaking His name is praise! Thank you, God, for the day!! I raise my head from my pillow in praise. I remember who you are which is a blessing! It is truly all I need for God is the creator of all mankind, higher than anything and anyone, outstanding any superstar filled with fame. Looking at Heaven and Earth, who has so majestic a palace as He? From horizon to horizon and morning to night, who sees and hears more than He or knows more than He? Who has more power and authority?

None can compare no matter how they try. He takes the least and makes them the greatest. He takes the forgotten and ignored to raise to the heights. He gives children to those who seek joy for this is His way. What do you desire of God? Remember who He is. That is your blessing! That is the answer to your dreams. He remembers His promises and His blessings are always fulfilled. So, to all who serve God, just speak His name as praise and remember who His is. He's the same God. Go outside. Survey His majesty. Remember who He is and that is your blessing for when you remember who He is, your prayers will be answered. He is the same yesterday, today and forever. Look at the sunflower as it lifts its head to the morning sun remembering who God is. Lift yourself to His Son and remember who God is.

God makes everything come out right; he puts victims back on their feet. He showed Moses how he went about his work, opened up his plans to all Israel. God is sheer mercy and grace; not easily angered, He's rich in love. He doesn't endlessly nag and scold, nor hold grudges forever. He doesn't treat us as our sins deserve, nor pay us back in full for our wrongs. As high as heaven is over the earth, so strong is his love to those who fear him. And as far as sunrise is from sunset, he has separated us from our sins. As parents feel for their children, God feels for those who fear him. He knows us inside and out, keeps in mind that we're made of mud. Men and women don't live very long; like wildflowers they spring up and blossom, But a storm snuffs them out just as quickly, leaving nothing to show they were here. God's love, though, is ever and always, eternally present to all who fear him, Making everything right for them and their children as they follow his Covenant ways and remember to do whatever he said.
Psalms 103:6-18

Why God?

On a day like today, why choose God?

From Psalms 103 (then from me)

He forgives your sins—everyone. (Yes, those that others see and don't see because He sees/knows all)

He heals your diseases—everyone. (Your timetable isn't His, but healing is his specialty)

He redeems you from hell—saves your life! (A lake of fire where you constantly burn or a place of eternal rest by cool water-your choice)

He crowns you with love and mercy—a paradise crown. (Like being a princess or prince? - I mean like being showered with mercy & love??)

He wraps you in goodness—beauty eternal. (No night creme necessary-just constant beauty)

He renews your youth—you're always young in his presence. (Age has no factor in His eyes-He makes all things new!)

God makes everything come out right.

he puts victims back on their feet. (He's the victor and he fight your battles for you)

He showed Moses how he went about his work, (He will show you too if you ask)

He opened up his plans to all Israel. (Even though they treated Him badly-even killed His son)

God is sheer mercy and grace; (I mean who doesn't want pure mercy and grace when you mess up like all the time?)

He's not easily angered, (This is like a miracle because some of these people are pure idiots-whoops-shouldn't say that!)

He's rich in love. (Love holds more wealth than the dollar-which is falling like a rock!)

He doesn't endlessly nag and scold, (Hey guys...wanna know someone who accepts you as you are without complaint?)

He doesn't hold grudges forever. (Now this is pretty cool-because some of these folks...well...)

He doesn't treat us as our sins deserve, (I'll just leave this here with no extra comments!)

He doesn't pay us back in full for our wrongs. (how cool is this? You know we deserve it too!)

As high as heaven is over the earth, so strong is his love to those who fear him. (Fear as in Respect not cringe)

And as far as sunrise is from sunset, he has separated us from our sins. (Yea, remember that not paying you back part earlier...)

As parents feel for their children, God feels for those who fear him. (The good kinda parent not the stinky kind!)

He knows us inside and out, (best thing ever because I don't have to be FB perfect)

He keeps in mind that we're made of mud. (Well now...I know you were made of that stinky kind, but he made me of that pretty colored clay-the one that sparkles-Just kidding!)

People do not live exceptionally long; like wildflowers they spring up and blossom, But a storm snuffs them out just as quickly, leaving nothing to show they were here. (Ouch-that is a little rough statement there-women live longer than men though on average-just saying!)

God's love, though, is ever and always, eternally present to all who fear him, (wow! He never forgets to show it either...that is the best part! He does not forget birthdays nor notable events either-always shows up!)

He always Making everything right for us and our children as we follow his Covenant ways and remember to do whatever he said. (wow, we get a rule book, we get mercy, we get forgiveness, and we get everything made right...super cool!)

God has set his throne in heaven; he rules over us all. (Yea, and He's like made us the coolest mansions too...one that matches exactly to you)

He is the King! (And we get to be the King's kids with all the benefits!)

So, bless God, you angels, ready and able to fly at his bidding, quick to hear and do what he says. (Yea-you all angels better get busy you hear!)

Bless God, all you armies of angels, alert to respond to whatever he wills. (Yea, when He asks on my behalf-jump to it-do not be late please)

Bless God, all creatures, wherever you are— everything and everyone made by God. (This means you all the pretty birds and butterflies and even you ugly bugs too and the rocks, trees, and wind...)

And you, O my soul, bless God!" (So, this is my part? All I gotta do is bless God for the win-sign me up-ready to do my part!)

Don't be in any rush to become a teacher, my friends. Teaching is highly responsible work. Teachers are held to the strictest standards. And none of us is perfectly qualified. We get it wrong nearly every time we open our mouths. If you could find someone whose speech was perfectly true, you'd have a perfect person, in perfect control of life. A bit in the mouth of a horse controls the whole horse. A small rudder on a huge ship in the hands of a skilled captain sets a course in the face of the strongest winds. A word out of your mouth may seem of no account, but it can accomplish nearly anything- or destroy it! It only takes a spark, remember, to set off a forest fire. A careless or wrongly placed word out of your mouth can do that. By our speech we can ruin the world, turn harmony to chaos, throw mud on a reputation, send the whole world up in smoke and go up in smoke with it, smoke right from the pit of hell. This is scary: You can tame a tiger, but you can't tame a tongue--it's never been done. The tongue runs wild, a wanton killer. With our tongues we bless God our Father; with the same tongues we curse the very men and women he made in his image. Curses and blessings out of the same mouth! My friends, this can't go on. A spring doesn't gush fresh water one day and brackish the next, does it? Apple trees don't bear strawberries, do they? Raspberry bushes don't bear apples, do they? You're not going to dip into a polluted mud hole and get a cup of clear, cool water, are you?
James 3:1-10

A Careless Rush!

Water rushing over ice formed these "eggs" of ice looking like pebbles but instead are hard rocks of ice that will melt in the sun. Like irresponsible words, these rocks of ice seem to be what they are not. A perfect speech given by a great orator often lasts the course of time as words of wisdom to live by and yet these God breathed words scripted by a mere fisherman bring more salve than many a perfected word. A word from your lips can accomplish many things both good and evil. A careless word can be like a spark that sets a blaze of a home or life while a well-placed word can change a relationship for the better. When my boys were little, I would tell them that people only use ugly words when they lack the vocabulary to express their thoughts. I wanted them to learn to use good language. I'll never forget the day one if my son's teachers called me through the intercampus phone and said I'm leaning over behind my desk because your son is telling me someone is having flatulence and I have no idea what he is talking about....it tickled me because he was reporting that a student was having gas but using his vocabulary. His previous teacher had called me requesting me to explain that "dam" was a bad word because when his dad went to work on the dam at NO during Katrina and he told his classmates, they all thought he had said a bad word...the language we use defines us. One of my favorite movies, My Fair Lady, is based on the premise that your vernacular can change the course of your life and I believe this. Your words have the power of life and death. You can speak uplifting truth or depressing facts about the same cup of water determining it to be one-half full or one-half empty. It is easy to get discouraged in your situation especially when it is not as you'd like it to be. It is just as easy to encourage yourself in God in these situations as this is what David told us to do. He said in situations that are discouraging we are to delight ourselves in The Lord. Delighting requires us to count the blessings.

But now, God's Message, the God who made you in the first place, Jacob, the One who got you started, Israel: "Don't be afraid, I've redeemed you. I've called your name. You're mine.
When you're in over your head, I'll be there with you. When you're in rough waters, you will not go down. When you're between a rock and a hard place, it won't be a dead end
Because I am God, your personal God, The Holy of Israel, your Savior. I paid a huge price for you: all of Egypt, with rich Cush and Seba thrown in! That's how much you mean to me! That's how much I love you! I'd sell off the whole world to get you back, trade the creation just for you.
Isaiah 43:1-4

The Truth is...!

I do not like water except in a hot bath.
I do not like conflict except when I have no choice.
I do like chocolate but only on occasion.
My favorite drink is peach tea but even that I get sick of sometimes.
I am super emotional a lot but rarely show my intensity of feelings until I explode (warning: steroids make emotional roller coaster worse as does tension).
I am far from perfect, but I dream of being better.
I am thankful for my husband & family, neighbors, friends, church family and amazing employees & colleagues who bear my burdens with me.
I am harder on my family than on others.
I am harder on my body than I should be.
I am highly demanding as a person and have grand expectations of those around me that are often unrealistic and unreasonable. (My staff secretly calls me the tornado/hurricane-they love my shirt that says I am a little sunshine mixed in with hurricane because it is truth)
I am lazy and unmotivated but internally a lot but rarely still or at rest. My mind is always going.
In pain, your true colors show and mine are often not pretty.
I am mouthy and say too much. I am a hindrance to myself often.
I am ashamed of how I act often, and I must repent and ask for forgiveness often. I am sorry isn't enough.
I am scared of the truth about me. And I am in love with The Truth of Him.
I am relieved that the God who made me,
. I am amazed that God redeemed me.
I am blessed that He called me by name.
I am thrilled that He chose me.
I am often in over my head but when I am, He is with me. I am in tough situations and rough waters a lot, but He does not let me drown.
When I reach up to Him, He pulls me close and walks on the waters with me.
When I get caught between the rock and the hard place (known as the truth of me and my situation which is what I must live with in a seemingly impossible place) I know that I can cling to The Rock and He will hold me through it because He is my hiding place, refuge and personal God.
The Truth is He paid a huge price for me. He loves me like no other.
I do not have to rely on the feelings and opinions of others around me, but I can lean into Him.
Jesus is the answer! Lord, take these burdens & do what only you can do!

Now God has us where he wants us, with all the time in this world and the next to shower grace and kindness upon us in Christ Jesus. Saving is all his idea, and all his work. All we do is trust him enough to let him do it. It's God's gift from start to finish! We don't play the major role. If we did, we'd probably go around bragging that we'd done the whole thins! No, we neither make nor save ourselves. God does both the making and saving. He creates each of us by Christ Jesus to join him in the work he does, the good work he has gotten ready for us to do, work we had better be doing.
Ephesians 2:7-10

Time is on our side!

Time marches on, Time flies.... A Stitch in Time Saves Nine. ...Time Is Precious. ...Time Is on My Side. ...At a Set Time. ...and many more sayings abound about time because it is one thing, we have little control over and yet we strive to do so. God controls time and all that happens in each minute of each day, but we like to think that we are the managers of that time when in reality we grasp so little of it. The brain cannot fathom the word forever or infinity because it cannot define it...just like it cannot fathom God...He does not fit in our box of time. He is not defined by our limits nor our clocks.

There is not much more frustrating than waiting on something or someone for an in-determinate period of time because we are bound by finite bonds. We like to measure with our own measures, but scripture tells us that a day with the Lord is as a thousand years.... imagine.... this earth formed thousands of years ago according to man's timetable only a few days ago by God's. Mind boggling! Our entire lifespan is only minutes in God's time and yet so much we waste on petty things. God wrote the script, created the set and the players and He is the main character who has the stage. We merely have a minor role and yet...He takes time to rewrite the script for those minutes we play because we ask, and He answers. So cool! Our role is simply to follow His lead and play our part trusting Him to take care of us.

Don't be naive. There are difficult times ahead. As the end approaches, people are going to be self-absorbed, money hungry, self-promoting, stuck-up, profane, contemptuous of parents, crude, coarse, dog-eat-dog, unbending, slanderers, impulsively wild, savage, cynical, treacherous, ruthless, bloated windbags, addicted to lust, and allergic to God. They'll make a show of religion, but behind the scenes they're animals.
Stay clear of these people.
2 Timothy 3:1-5

Fazed!

Don't let it faze you! Wow! Our world is shaking and quaking on its foundations and God says, "Be still."

Fazed. Shocked. Shaken. Stressed. Hurting. Angry. Upset. All emotions. Paul writes to Timothy...you were raised in God's love and knowledge...from the time you were born...you know Him...and His promises so stay the course. Quit letting life get your goat! You know the truth! You know Him intimately so why are you leaving what you know for the uncertainty? Life is unpredictable but God is the same forever. God has a plan for us...we must trust. Every day and everywhere I hear of the uncertainty, but I know. I don't know about tomorrow, but I know whom holds me. I know Him. Security comes from knowing because knowing allows trusting. Trust is the first step of faith. The introduction to faith is in the knowing. Tomorrow may be filled with uncertainty, but it is also filled with possibilities and promise. I would rather walk into a day of uncertainty filled with promise and possibility than to walk into a known circumstance without possibility and promise.

Therefore humble yourselves
under the mighty hand of God, that He may
exalt you in due time, casting all your care upon
Him, for He cares for you. Be sober, be vigilant;
because your adversary the devil walks about
like a roaring lion, seeking whom he may
devour. Resist him, steadfast in the faith,
knowing that the same sufferings are
experienced by your brotherhood in the world.
But may the God of all grace, who called us to
His eternal glory by Christ Jesus, after you have
suffered a while, perfect, establish, strengthen,
and settle you. To Him be the glory and the
dominion forever and ever. Amen.
1 Peter 5:6-11

Content in Him!

Resistance is a natural reaction to things that make you uncomfortable or unhappy, scared, or anxious because this is the human fight or flight reaction. Babies scream, toddlers throw fits, teenagers throw things and adults do all three but usually less obviously. When they disagree on FB, they post negative comments or angry faces or unfollow/unfriend. When they feel these things in person, they scream, yell, throw fits, say things they don't mean or those with self-control, walk away...sometimes they walk away permanently in our lives. Suffer isn't fun and it's hard to be going through things that bring hardship and frustration but if we pay attention to God's word, He tells us to resist these reactions and hold steadfast to the faith we know. He says He uses these sufferings for a little while to perfect us, to strengthen us, to establish us and to settle us. When babies are first born, everything makes them fussy then they become acquainted with minor things, and they don't fuss as much.

They start having a better perception of true pain versus wet pain. As they grow up, they begin to understand the difference in not getting my way pain and real suffering to some extent. Whenever my back or other things start bothering me, I try to put it in perspective to what I see others suffering...it sheds a whole new light. I'm not suffering broken bones or a burned body, just a few muscle and nerve pains. I've had a setback but I'm not completely down. You see, the devil wants us to get down and dirty into the fit throwing toddler stage where we rage at God because when we are raging and allowing our anger to take hold, we lash out at everyone around us ruining relationships and separating ourselves from the love of God...that's how prey is captured. First, it must be separated from the herd...pulled away from church, at angst with family, pulled into oneself so that he can start the deciduous work of deception and killing of the spirit. This tug of war and frustration at everyone and everything around us is his tool along with fear because he knows our human reaction of flight/fight means we will either rage against God and family or we will flee God's word and His people...either of which allows him to win points...it is only when we overcome by God's word and the power of our testimony that we win. When we trust God no matter how dire the circumstances, God raises us up. Yes, we may suffer a little while...it may even seem like forever...but even during that suffering He is making us stronger. He is building our faith and working a beautiful work.

Greater is He that is in me than he that is of this world. Read Job. The devil had to ask God for permission to harm Job and take from him. God allowed it to work within Job and yes, he suffered the loss of his children. It was devastating. He lost everything that we measure success by in this world...even his spouse turned on him but God. God was always there, and Job knew it even when he couldn't feel him. He knew God. He had relationship. No one can give you this. It takes work, willingness, and persistence. But God. If your circumstances have you down, say aloud But God....say it repeatedly...until you have the faith to conquer your circumstances...but God...will wipe away every tear, will restore, will provide...But God...say it again.

I will give you a new heart and put a new spirit within you; I will take the heart of stone out of your flesh and give you a heart of flesh. I will put My Spirit within you and cause you to walk in My statutes, and you will keep My judgments and do them. Then the nations which are left all around you shall know that I, the Lord, have rebuilt the ruined places and planted what was desolate. I, the Lord, have spoken it, and I will do it."
Ezekiel 36:26-27, 36

Despite It ALL!

Interesting that in this passage, God tells Ezekiel to prophesy to the mountains not to the people. In His word, He says that if we do not acknowledge Him, the rocks will cry out His praise. In these words, Ezekiel is speaking a promise over the people not because they have done as God directed or even because they deserved it but rather in spite of it. Despite their lack of loyalty and despite their iniquities, God speaks a promise over their lives because of His honor and His loyalty to them. God is speaking promises over our lives every day if we will but listen to them and pay attention. Too often we get wrapped up in the mode of what is happening, and we fail to recognize that His promises are at work within us, working out what we cannot see! Despite us, God is working for us. Despite our lack of faith, despite our lack or belief and trust, despite our desire to go through the hard times…Despite it all, HE has made His promises and even though we cannot see and we are less than perfect, He is working a good thing in us to the going on of His kingdom. Never forget that we are His and here for His purpose!

Peter said, "Change your life. Turn to God and be baptized, each of you, in the name of Jesus Christ, so your sins are forgiven. Receive the gift of the Holy Spirit. The promise is targeted to you and your children, but also to all who are far away-whomever, in fact, Our Master God invites."
Acts 2:38-39

The Promise!

Repent, change your life, turn to God, be baptized so your sins may be forgiven. Peter's words still ring the echo of Jesus Christ through the centuries but so many stop there. They are genuinely sorry and give their all to Jesus in their walk but fail to receive the promise. The eternal hope brought by salvation is an enormous gift of portend but it isn't The Promise! You see when Jesus ascended to Heaven, He gave a promise to send the Holy Spirit to dwell with us as a comforter and friend until His return...this was His Promise but many fail to wait to receive the promise. They are satisfied with the main course and skip the wait for the dessert. They miss out on the fulfilling gift of His Spirit. I love the beach for its beauty, but I must admit I'm a chicken of the waves as I don't enjoy swimming. I love to look at the water and I like to swim in my pool but the vastness of the ocean uncontainable gives me shivers.

When I think of the ocean in terms of God, this is how we are so timid. We want to walk along the beach with Him and let Him carry us through the tough spots, but we are unwilling to go deeper and trust Him to lift us above the waves. When we wade out into His love and the waves of His presence surround us, overwhelm us, we bask in His glory, and He lifts us up...the promise of His spirit within us is fulfilled. As I watched my kids in the river this past week playing, kayaking, swimming, and fishing...they had a freedom...an abandonment of fear and containment that I honestly envied as I clung to the shore. They laughed and splashed...they had a freedom that was unlimited...this is what I want in Christ.

I want to wade out into the ocean of His love and allow His spirit to overwhelm me, drown me in His presence so that my life becomes His...that my being be swallowed up into freedom of life and not bound by external means. I want to be more like Him in everything I do and speak. I want to be just like Him walking in the Promise of His Spirit within me. The Master has invited us to walk on the waters with Him. He has given us His Promise, but we must receive it. Isn't it time you left the shoreline and waded out into His fullness?

He told them, "You don't get to know the time. Timing is the Father's business. What you'll get is the Holy Spirit. And when the Holy Spirit comes on you, you will be able to be my witnesses in Jerusalem, all over Judea and Samaria, even to the ends of the world." These were his last words. As they watched, he was taken up and disappeared in a cloud. They stood there, staring into the empty sky.

Suddenly two men appeared in white robes! They said, "You Galileans!-why do you just stand here looking up at an empty sky? This very Jesus who was taken up from among you to heaven will come as certainly and mysteriously as he left."

Acts 1:7-11

It's About Time!

Frantically rushing and trying to meet a schedule of something takes up a lot of our lives. We become a slave to time as it dictates our waking and sleeping but also most of our day. On our trip, we were staying on the time zone which was interesting because in one part of the property it was central time zone and another it was eastern...talk about brain training...we were constantly having to say central or eastern because as we planned our days we had to adhere to a schedule of whichever timezone the activity was in..this my favorite part of the day was the morning when time had no say...I could wake up and just chill with my tea and The Word in a beautiful setting that He created. So completely refreshing. There is such freedom in the times of no schedule.

Jesus' words.... you don't get to know the time...put a whole spin on things. a mystery...He left the control of schedule and timing out of our hands because He knew we were prone to allow time to become our Master. As He was taken in the clouds, the mystery was there and continues...He is coming soon but we don't know the day or time because He doesn't want us limited to time...He wants us to be witnesses wherever we are and in all situations. He puts people in your path for the purpose of His timing. He gives you opportunity and ministry in your daily tasks, but you must be willing to open the door to the view. This view this morning was a gorgeous cloud shaped like a hand over the mountains...the colors from the sun even painted it the color of skin...it was like the hand of God reaching out to the mountains putting on the perfect touch...Jesus said He's coming again in clouds of glory to gather His people and we will meet Him in the air...could it be today?

Absolutely, come quickly Lord Jesus! Meanwhile we are chosen to be filled with His Holy Spirit and to be witnesses in caverns and on mountaintops. Yesterday I had the privilege of being His hand extended into a life in a cavern. You never know where He will use you or His gifts. Be alert. Be ready. Ask for Him to touch you and quicken your heart with His spirit when He is putting someone in your path...it will be through Him. The road before you may seem long and weary but if you look to the Master Creator who is the Master of Time rather than being rushed by the scheduling of the day...you will find that the days become a mystery of who rather than a rat race. Who will God put in my path today? Is it you?

It is absolutely clear that God has called you to a free life. Just make sure that you don't use this freedom as an excuse to do whatever you want to do and destroy your freedom. Rather, use your freedom to serve one another in love; that's how freedom grows.For everything we know about God's Word is summed up in a single sentence: Love others as you love yourself. That's ah act of true freedom. If you bite and ravage each other, watch out -in no time at all you will be annihilating each other, and where will your precious freedom be then?
Galatians 5:13-15

Freedom through service!

Freedom is often taken for granted until you no longer have it. As children we don't understand boundaries until they are defined by the playpen, then the fenced yard, then rules and instructions then laws. But freedom always comes at a price. When people are free, they don't use freedom as an excuse to harm others or contain others. True freedom is in the heart. It's a state of mind. An absolutely free person has no problem serving others because they understand that acts of service done in love lead to more freedom. Yesterday we traveled deep into a cave and the lights were turned out. I have never been in a place so dark in all my life. The guide was telling us while we were standing in the dark about the Chilean miners and their 169 days in the tunnels with no light. They survived only because they had each other to lean on and when they finally achieved freedom from the rubble, they had an inner freedom that has followed them despite the obstacles in vision and such they have to overcome. Freedom is a fragile thing that requires tending. It is built on service, sacrifice, and love. Selfish desires destroy this freedom. When the guide shared with us how the caves were discovered and showed us the tiny hole these men go into to go wild caving...I thought there is no way.... but freedom isn't just going your own way but a willingness to lay yourself down for others.

A freedom in God is true freedom and is achieved by serving others. Seek first the kingdom of God then Freedom comes. Christ made the sacrifice that gives us freedom from the bondage of sin as well as freedom from the bondage of fear, death, hell, and the grave.... but we must accept His nail scarred hand of sacrifice to embrace the true freedom. Clinging to self and our own ways keeps us from the wonderful freedom gained through service to others. As the guide closed our tour, he told us the story of the cave explorers. They were willing to lay it all on the line to find the caves...they had to trust one another to push and pull them through narrow crevices and many failed to survive but they laid down their lives to discover. There are lots of distinct types of freedom but there is none so rewarding as that of a person willing to sacrifice their own desires to bless another. Laying down life to take up a heart of loving sacrifice. Greater love has no man than to lay down his (selfish, prideful wants and desires) life in love for another. The sad thing I see today is all the biting and tearing at others. One cannot achieve freedom by destroying others. They will instead destroy themselves and lose their own freedom. Lord, let us see your ways and not our own.

Those who think they can do it on their own end up obsessed with measuring their own moral muscle but never get around to exercising it in real life. Those who trust God's action in them find that God's Spirit is in them-living and breathing God! Obsession with self in these matters is a dead end; attention to God leads us out into the open, into a spacious, free life. Focusing on the self is the opposite of focusing on God.

Anyone completely absorbed in self ignores God, ends up thinking more about self than God. That person ignores who God is and what he is doing. And God isn't pleased at being ignored.

Romans 8:5-8

Obsessed!

She dove repeatedly at my head obsessed with getting me away from her nest and I unrelenting pressed on unaware of why she kept circling and diving towards me intent on getting away from her. The closer I came to the nest the more agitated she became and the more aggressive she became, the more I rushed in the direction she was trying to get me to avoid. This osprey and I could not communicate because each of us was obsessed with our own purpose and neither saw the issue with clarity. Finally, Wes said she has a nest up ahead with babies in it. She's protecting her little ones and she sees you as a threat. Her nest was right in the area I was headed and as soon as I passed it by going in a different direction, she flew into the nest and sat.

The saying goes "you gotta walk the walk and not just talk the talk" or better put "you gotta walk the talk". Faith isn't faith until it's in action. That's when it grows. Beginning faith is the faith of salvation but deep faith is the faith that has been walked. You don't ask someone who is brand new at their job how to do better at yours, you ask someone who has been there...someone who knows from experience because the walking is the experience. When Wes told me what was happening with the osprey, I knew he knew because he had been in nature as a game warden for over 20 years and as a hunter many years prior and since. I trust him in all things with nature and water and outdoors because he knows that stuff.

God knows that stuff. God knows our stuff. He sent his son to walk the talk so He could express to us that He knows not just because He is God and our creator but because He lived it, died for us, and rose again conquering it all. It is so easy to talk it but harder still to walk in it. The key is trust. Paul was writing to the Romans who lived an extravagant lifestyle much like we do in America. They liked to talk about it, but they were self-absorbed only seeing their own circumstances and refusing to see the whole picture. When you are living and breathing God, there is a sense of freedom and openness to breathe, dream and stretch out to the impossible. Peter focused on Jesus and walked on water but when he focused on himself and his fear/inability, he began to sink. We all move in/out of places of trust/fear in different circumstances but when we rise above it, then we soar.

The osprey got tired of diving at my head and soared a little higher which changed her perspective because then she could see I was too small to be a threat and I was moving away instead of towards...when my back was to her, her trust factor kicked in and she sat on her nest once again. But when I turned towards the nest again on my way back, she soared high...she didn't dive bomb me. She was watchful and cautious, but she moved in more freedom because she had a better measure of me that she could trust. God wants us to trust completely so we can soar completely free, but it is up to us. We can stumble around in our own moral morass trying to fit everyone's opinion into our way or we can simply trust God. Let him walk the talk with us because He has already been here and experienced it all even to death which He conquered through Christ Jesus. It's our choice: walking in freedom with Him in complete trust or walking in the fearful unknown of selfish desires. God isn't pleased at being ignored so He demands attention through life.

"Here is a simple rule of thumb for behavior: Ask yourself what you want people to do for you; then grab the initiative and do it for them! If you only love the lovable, do you expect a pat on the back? Run-of-the-mill sinners do that.
If you only help those who help you, do you expect a medal? Garden-variety sinners do that. If you only give for what you hope to get out of it, do you think that's charity? The stinsiest of pawnbrokers does that. "I tell you, love your enemies. Help and give without expecting a return. You'll never I promise regret it. Live out this God-created identity the way our Father lives toward us, generously and graciously, even when we're at our worst. Our Father is kind; you be kind.
Luke 6:31-36

Rule of Thumb!

It is a beautiful ivy but is an invasive species. I look at it through this window and see its beauty, but I also see how it has taken over everything between me and the river. Its behavior is predictable because it has a pattern of choking the life out of all the plants around it as it climbs the trees and smothers them. Beauty isn't always beneficial just like complimentary things are not always in your favor. A rule of thumb is a pattern of behavior. What is mine? Can people predict how I will react? Do I follow a pattern of Christ or am I a pattern of selfishness? It's easy to love the lovable because they are easy. It's hard to love those who are prickly because they have thorns warning you off, each representing a previous hurt. These thorns surround the roses in their life but too often we fail to surround them with love despite the thorns and instead we pull back when we get poked allowing the world around to choke and smother them with their cultural policies. I think it's significant that Christ Jesus wore a crown of thorns. It symbolizes the cultural approach to Christ. The culture is fully mocking him, bringing Him immense pain and maximum drama as the blood poured from his head. Those thorns represented the disdain that mankind had for the Savior of the world. The church today has embraced the culture and like the kudzu...the world is choking the message of Christ in the church. The mockery is that how we ourselves treat others will ultimately be our demise. Jesus tells us that the measure of our behavior-the rule of thumb-should be the initiative of love towards the unlovable.

Who is unlovable in your life? Think of the thing that you would like to be blessed with...and bless them! Want to have amazing relationships? Treat others with an important level of servanthood, bless them, and lift them up! The rule of thumb is kindness! Do everything you do out of love. Be kind to those who despitefully use you. Want to achieve your dreams? Do unto others as you wish God your Father to do for you!

How do you stop an invasive plant that is taking over everything? You manage it with the proper tools. You cut off the roots in the areas of your life where you don't want it to spread and you allow it to thrive in the area where it dwells...eventually, it will choke itself out. I watch the churches around me being choked by the culture they have embraced and mocked in the public politics. I see that the kudzu got its hold on these, and they look beautiful, but they are dying while the culture chokes them. Jesus tells us to do well in love and kindness. This means to be loving and kind but also beware. The lawnmower just came by and cut the invasive thread of the vine back...before it reaches the house and the protected plants. This is done in full awareness that without this line being held, this species would take over. Loving kindness doesn't mean open acceptance. It means that by demonstrating the love of the Father and holding the line of truth in kindness, we can exist in this world to bring light into the darkness. I smile because I reflect on the fireflies flittering through the kudzu last night. They freely flew through, dancing around the creeping vines, uninhibited by the false beauty. This is us. We are the church of Christ...the bride...called to stand and hold a line in kindness and love but free to fly in unencumbered with His presence in the darkness as a beacon to those who are lost.

So, chosen by God for this new life of love, dress in the Wardrobe God picked out for you: compassion, kindness, humility, quiet strength, discipline. Be even-tempered, content with second place, quick to forgive an offense. Forgive as quickly and completely as the Master forgave you. And regardless of what else you put on, wear love. It's your basic, all-purpose garment. Never be without it.
Colossians 3:12-14

The Must Have Garment!

When visiting Ruby Falls, the love story behind the history is very compelling of a young man who left his home to follow his girl and made his fortune by discovering/excavating a cave where the falls are located. The falls aren't Ruby as you might surmise but rather that was the name of his girl, Ruby! This particular picture is called Ruby's drapery and mirror because her beau/husband at that point said it reminded him of her...that's sweet love.

Love is more than the little black dress which you can wear dressed up or down wherever you go. Love is an inner garment that wraps you securely and shows your best assets without revealing too much! Love is the undergarment that makes the outer garments look great. The outer garments are compassion, kindness, humility, quiet strength, and discipline. God even included the footwear we should choose even temper, contentedness, and forgiveness. Just picture this mirror reflection of a person encased in love with a beautiful outerwear of quietness and footwear of contentedness. That's the picture God wanted us to see.
He chose the perfect things for you, but I remember laying out clothes for my kids to wear and them refusing to wear them. Sometimes that is what happens to us. Specifically, I remember Gabriel always wanting to wear the "Mr. Charles" shirt to church. On one particular Sunday, by happenstance, I dressed Gabriel in a button up plaid and when we arrived at Sunday School, he matched Charles Walker whom he adored...they were both redheads and Charles...well he always wears God's undergarment of love. Anyway, after that Sunday, I could never get Gabriel to wear any other shirt to church until he graduated Charles' class because there was always a chance, he could match Charles again. You see as a child; he recognized the garments of God's love and he wanted to be like that. Scripture tells us to be as a child. It tells us to put on the garments of praise, garments of love...it shows us that these are choices.

We don't have to walk in disappointments and bitterness...throw those black garments off and walk in the garments of love and shoes of contentedness. Your life may be perfectly blessed, and you are excited to dress for the party of life or your life can stink and have nothing but either way, you still have the same garments available to you. God has provided you the clothes and shoes to wear but you must choose to dress in those. Whenever I get dressed up in my finery, I always feel a little glamorous and uplifted but the truth is my undergarments are the same whether I am in glitz n glam or my old faithfuls. That's what God is trying to tell us...the undergarments of love should be on you always...followed by the outerwear of faith, kindness, gentleness, etc. but we must choose. We are not infants that must be dressed but rather children whose Father has laid our clothes and told us to get dressed. Time to wake up! Get dressed as He has instructed and go about your day in His apparel.

It's threaded with the finest gold of His anointing and scented with His fragrance so that others will be drawn to His presence. If it's raining, put on the raincoat of praise, because praising in the storms breaks chains of bondage and calms the frightening.

The soul of a lazy man desires, and has nothing;But the soul of the diligent shall be made rich.

Righteousness guards him whose way is blameless But wickedness overthrows the sinner.

The light of the righteo rejoices, But the lamp of the wicked will be put put out

The righteous eats to the satisfying of his soul,But the stomach of the wicked shall be in want.
Proverbs 13:4, 6, 9,25

The Work of Righteousness!

Did you know your soul must work? Most people passively realize it but rarely put work into it and this is a kingdom key. There are two types of righteousness discussed in scripture. The first type is Corum Deo which is faith filled righteousness of God himself incarnated into you for salvation...by faith you are saved not by works lest any man should boast. This requires only the faith to believe and confess then Jesus' sacrifice covers all your sins leading to righteousness through Him, but we should note what is said in Proverbs. The soul of a lazy man wants but has nothing while the soul of the diligent is rich...this describes the fact that the soul must work at the second type of righteousness which is Corum Mundo, the work of the moral man in relationship to others.

Righteousness guards him whose way is blameless...meaning if one does nothing to deserve punishment then no punishment is given, and the soul rejoices. The reality is we can walk a sinless life and still not have everything we want because we are not walk in diligence to those around us. Our righteousness or moral compasses are but filthy rags when compared to Jesus' blood. The Pharisees and Sadducees of Jesus' day were the political religious parties. They took sides and pulled/tugged the people to get on their side of the issues much like we see today when religion and politics collide. The diligent work of the soul is to align with Christ not a certain church group, political campaign nor moral stance. Righteousness must be trained and fed. If you are constantly feeding on the fodder of the world and not diving deep into His word, it's like getting sawdust instead of steak. Your body and soul get no value and cannot grow nor effectively minister to others.

This photo is of Lover's Leap atop Lookout Mountain near Chattanooga, TN (actually in GA). The story is of a young Native American man captured and thrown from this cliff to his death for his perceived crimes and his girl leaped to her death after him because she couldn't live without him. The beautiful waterfall supposedly symbolizes their everlasting love as it flows. This is a man told story of uncertain origin with the soul of one unable to survive without the other...what if we longed for God's righteousness as she longed for her lover. Are we willing to fling our physical needs, desires and wants aside to be in His righteousness.
Yesterday I kept trying to clean my glasses with my shirt, a rag, a paper towel and even a glass cloth but could only see smudges. I was getting so frustrated...I washed them with soap, then Windex, then used a perfect cloth...still there was a large smudge every-time I looked through them. Then I went and looked in the mirror at them.
The smudge was on my eye itself...a part of my mascara was on my eye and when I put on my glasses, it smeared on there like a grease slick. The point is that I was so focused on what was wrong with my glasses that I failed to see the true problem until I had a reflection. Right now, as I type these words, the sun is hitting the river at just the right angle refracting the light into my eyes. While it stings and my eyes object, it clarifies and widens the view. This is the job of scripture which is a refractive perspective of God sending His words into our lives. So, the soul work we must do is to strive to Christ's righteousness. He is our moral compass.not our opinion of Him and not our opinion of His word...Him himself. HE is our moral compass! HE is our righteousness!

Greater love has no one than this, than to lay down one's life for his friends. You are My friends if you do whatever I command you. No longer do I call you servants, for a servant does not know what his master is doing; but I have called you friends, for all things that I heard from My Father I have made known to you. You did not choose Me, but I chose you and appointed you that you should go and bear fruit, and that your fruit should remain, that whatever you ask the Father in My name He may give you. These things I command you, that you love one another.
John 15:13-17

Greater Love!

I love to think of my friends, and I have lots of them from all over the world but the ones who know me intimately are the ones who know my mind. The intimacy of close friends comes from time and effort. Just lately I have come to a stage in my life where I no longer allow "false" friends to speak negativity into my life. I decided that I cannot make that person better by my light alone. Instead, I will remove myself rather than allow that spirit to become a part of me. Jesus says a truth here that few wish to acknowledge; we are friends of Him only if we do as He instructed. If we are His friends, we know His mind and His heart. We know how we should treat others, act ourselves and how to be. When we are uncertain, He gave us His words and continues to guide us as we ask and life within His boundaries.

Recently Wes had to thin His garden because this way his plants could get the best. A set of fruit plants cane down with a bug or disease, and he had to pull them lest they infect the others. The point is that sometimes we must thin our influences because they are not speaking God's promises, love, and truths into our lives. They aren't bearing fruit but rather bringing disease, negativity, sickness, and pain. This doesn't mean we physically get rid of them necessarily because sometimes they are family or close relationships...instead we must begin to pray for them and let them go into God's care. I carry people...it's my nature and in doing so, get burned a lot. I enjoy relationships and intimacy, but God is showing me that there is enmity between people who are not walking in relationship with Him and I because of Him and that is a purpose because roots must grow deeper for the plant to grow so weeding is necessary. If I want to draw closer to Him, I must let them go into His care. I must allow my feelings to be safe in Him and not carried in my body. This is huge for me because pain and hurt internalizes. As I sit here typing this, I realize that the only person affected by my selfish act of carrying others has been me. I have not helped people in their relationship with God by carrying them but rather hindered a closer walk. I'm honestly not sure why God is having me share this today but perhaps you are carrying another person, concerned about their spiritual walk and their physical body. Perhaps you have invested all of yourself into them and they are not moving forward. It is time to let go. The river of life is moving, and you are trying to hold them to the dock of your presence. Maybe it's fear of losing them or fear of them getting ahead of you but God wants you to let them go and release them into His keeping. Continue to pray and intercede for them as He directs but allow God to speak and move in their lives and yours. As a mom, one of the hardest things as kids grow into adulthood is letting go but not losing connection. It's painfully hard but it is a part of life. This letting go is a process of growing closer to God. Let Go and Let God have His wonderful way...your troubles will vanish, your night turn today if you let go and let God.

Greater love has no one than this, than to lay down his life for a friend has a different meaning for me now. Not just be willing to give up my physical life for another but rather allowing God to be God and lay down my wants and desires in favor of what God has for my friends and family. Harder call...knowing the mind of God...frees you from the burden. Love.God's love requires us to know His mind and heart in this!